THE AVIATOR

the life and music of

Steve Morse

Adrian Jarvis

THE AVIATOR

the life and music of

Steve Morse

Adrian Jarvis

WP
WYMER PUBLISHING
Bedford, England

First published in 2025 by Wymer Publishing, Bedford, England
www.wymerpublishing.co.uk Tel: 01234 326691
Wymer Publishing is a trading name of Wymer (UK) Ltd.

Print edition (fully illustrated): **ISBN: 978-1-915246-74-5**

Edited by Jerry Bloom.

Printed and bound in Great Britain by
CMP, Dorset.

A catalogue record for this book is available from the British Library.

eBook formatting by Lin White at Coinlea Services.
Typeset/Design by Andy Bishop / Tusseheia Creative
Cover design: Tusseheia Creative.
Front & back cover photos: Bill O'Leary / Timeless Concert Images.

Contents

Prologue:
Here And Now And Then

The guitarist, who is also a pilot, says that music and flying have much in common. Both require training and skill. Both fire the imagination, test the creativity. And both are confrontations with the sublime, whether that be realised in the vastness of the sky or a perfect combination of notes. When the guitarist (who is also a pilot) picks up his instrument and hangs it around himself like a familiar coat, or, perhaps, some lost part of himself that is vital and needed, it is not so different from when he runs through a list of pre-flight checks. The anticipation is the same, the excitement is the same and the small, mostly suppressed, but still present, fear of failure is the same.

He takes a plectrum and moves it over and around the strings. Screeching sounds. Deep rumbles. Hard edged. It could be the spluttering of a propeller roused to action. Expert fingers adjust the volume control, check the effects boxes, pump the tremolo arm.

He is searching for the notes, searching for a groove.

Old riffs, old times, old tunes, come back to him...

Half-played. Twiddled.

A stream of musical consciousness.

Smoke on... take it off the... those nights at the Albert Hall... student days... sitting at the controls of the aeroplane... or is it 'airplane'? The aviator... Meeting Roger in North Carolina... on top of the world... jamming with the Russian president...

... Janine...

It begins to resolve itself into a song...

Take off!

The song of a life. The journey of a life. The life of the guitarist who is also a pilot. The life of Steve Morse.

That life is the life of a consummate musician. There is no doubt about that. Because music and flying are not the same for everyone. They are the same for him — and calling Morse's life a song, or a flight, is more than a mere conceit.

Most of those who know anything about him are likely to have discovered the music before the man. He possibly entered the consciousness of those of us based in the UK (and who are old enough) courtesy of a show on the BBC's Radio 1 that went out between 10pm and midnight every Friday throughout the '80s and was called, logically, *The Friday Rock Show*.

Introduced by the late great Tommy Vance, with his rich bass, vaguely mid-Atlantic, voice, it was a weekly night school for those who liked their music hard and heavy. Many a teenager listened to it through headphones while lying on their bed. It resurrected such half-forgotten acts as Greenslade, Chicken Shack and Molly Hatchet, while championing the so-called New Wave of British Heavy Metal, which gave — or inflicted upon — the world the likes of Demon Pact and Cloven Hoof. Of this brief period, only Magnum, Diamond Head and Sansom emerged relatively unscathed, while Iron Maiden were the ones who went on to achieve actual stardom.

Yet, the show's theme tune was strangely lacking in the same sensibilities. Yes, it began with some shredding that sounded not unlike a steel tube being repeatedly bashed against another steel tube, but it soon settled to a highly commercial, quite funky, riff and some way-down-the-frets guitar soloing that led it onto drum breaks and barnstorming calls-and-responses.

It was an instrumental track, which was fine, but it eschewed the usual structure of rock. It was not circular or repetitive. It moved through a developing argument, like a classical piece, or jazz. It came back to those riffs late on, but only to round everything off. It was not something that might be found on a rock album, much less a heavy rock album. It sounded more like what it was being used for — a soundtrack.

It was 'Take It Off The Top' by the Dixie Dregs and it was written by Steve Morse. It is arguably his best-known work, irrespective of the fame that he later achieved upon joining one of the bands that Mr Vance most frequently featured on his show.

It first appeared on the 1978 album *What If* and neatly encapsulates the sophistication and artistry of the Dregs' sound at that point, while highlighting a problem for any biographer of its composer. If this is the piece that the imagined tune-up — or pre-flight check — above leads to, what kind of story does it suggest? What kind of song is it?

Colin Hart, the former Deep Purple tour manager — with whom Morse worked extensively in the nineties and noughties — when asked whether he had any 'stories' (i.e.: gossip) about Morse, simply replied, 'Not really. He always had a guitar with him and practised everywhere, in cars, buses, planes. Dedicated!'[1]

The conductor Paul Mann, another of Morse's sometime collaborators, said of him, 'He was born with that instrument in his hands. I know a lot of classical musicians who envy that kind of relationship with an instrument.'[2]

Critics and commentators have agreed with these views. Pete Pardo, whose *Sea of Tranquility* website and YouTube channel has, in part, filled the gap left by *The Friday Rock Show*, described Morse as, 'a musicians' musician,' who 'can play just about any style, has a unique sound that is so recognisable and has left an undeniable mark on music.'[3]

Pardo, having met Morse, described him as 'humble' and 'fascinating', 'a normal guy who is obsessed with music and the art of playing guitar.'

To sum up, the song, or flight, of Morse's life is not likely to be decadent, overly experimental, edgy or dangerous. His biography is no Rock 'n' Roll Babylon. This is not someone who has devoted himself to the more excessive sides of his chosen profession. Drug busts? Compromising photographs? Dubious sexual relationships? Scandals? Sorry — nothing to see here! This is the story of a musician, one with an almost Mozartian focus. A genius? It would be nice to say so, but the word has lost much of its value. Once applied to the chosen few who could influence an entire epoch in science, culture or whichever occupation they happened to pursue, it is now used of anyone who can pot three pool balls in a row. In any case, it is doubtful that Morse would call himself a genius.

So, what about 'virtuoso'? Insofar as it can be taken to mean a musician who demonstrates excellence, technical skill and showmanship, it is apt. But there is another dimension that is relevant here, the mystery that the term denotes,[4] the connection between audience and performer that cannot be readily accounted for by reference to technique, however faultless that technique might be. As will become clear, Morse certainly meets these criteria.

Steve Morse, Virtuoso, is getting there, but the word cannot stand on its own. He may have broken out of relative obscurity courtesy of a classic British band, but he never went, so to speak, native. He was pancakes and maple syrup, not black pudding and fried egg. His previous gigs had been with not only the Dixie Dregs, but Kansas. His music touched on European classical traditions for sure, but it also took in blues, jazz, rock 'n' roll... genres that are unashamedly American.

Stephen Bentley-Klein, a composer who also crossed paths with Morse, said of him, 'To me, Steve has a bit more of a hippy mentality. He plays with a bit more swing [than a lot of rock guitarists].'[5] As this implies, everything about Morse says, 'American', from his accent to his look to his slightly goofy smile.

The song, or flight, of his life, then, is that of a virtuoso, but not the type that normally springs to mind when that word is bandied about. It's not about an overweight tenor in ill-fitting white tie, or a violinist who thinks that it is cool to drop his first name, not that sort of virtuoso. A virtuoso who wears jeans and a t-shirt and a sleeveless denim top.

An American virtuoso.

1.
Rising Power

Steve Morse finally quit Deep Purple on 23rd July 2022. It was the end of a twenty-eight-year journey during which he had co-written — and performed on — numerous albums, travelled the world, travelled it again and kept on travelling it until there was no more world left to travel. He had earned the applause of millions and the scorn of those — those few — who could never quite forget his illustrious predecessor and accept Morse for who he was. In that it covered a generation of human history, an era had almost literally come to an end.

Although Morse's departure was brought about by the most tragic of circumstances, there was more than a hint of its having been in the offing for a while. The immediate circumstances were that his wife, Janine, had developed stage four cancer and was fighting a desperate, uphill, battle against the disease. His public statement on the situation was brief, but characteristically heartfelt, 'I wish to thank the listeners who so strongly supported live music and turned every show from a dress rehearsal to a thundering, exciting experience. I'll miss everybody in the band and crew but being Janine's helper and advocate has made a real difference at many key points.'[6]

The band's joint press release was every bit as simple, but no doubt hid any number of private conversations behind the scenes, 'Steve will be greatly missed by [the] band, crew, management, record label and all those that had the pleasure of working with him over the years. Steve has always been hugely grateful for the support and love of Deep Purple fans across the globe.'[7]

The band's singer, Ian Gillan, hinted that the dignity and restraint of the various pronouncements were far from the full story, 'It would be wrong to comment on his personal circumstances;

suffice to say he's in a bad place right now but dealing with it bravely and as best he can.'[8]

In many ways, this moment epitomises much about Steve Morse as a person. The humility. The concern for others. And above all, the music. It is perhaps natural that his resignation announcement should at least mention what he had been doing with the band, but it came with an addendum: bowing out of Deep Purple and full-on retirement were not one and the same. He reassured fans that he would still be performing and was already planning gigs with other collaborators. It was all really a question of scale: the vast expectation, never mind workload, associated with being a member of one of the world's biggest bands was what he was leaving behind, not music. Certainly not that. Music, after all, was his life.

It had always been there, from the moment that, that life had begun, on 28th July 1954, in Hamilton, Ohio. In that the town was named in honour of a man who has gone on to provide the inspiration for one of Broadway's most successful musicals, this could be called serendipitous.

In other respects, it was an inauspicious place to begin the Morse story. Photographs of it from around the time are artefacts of a long-vanished suburban America. The streets are as straight as the neck of a guitar and arranged in the grids that are the luxury of young civilisations, but which, nonetheless, speak of order and neighbourliness. Cars can be seen here and there, but small-town America is often full of emptiness and Hamilton in the fifties was no exception.

Every day was a quiet day. The central area was home to the kind of grand modern buildings that cannot have had a great deal of practical purpose for so small a population, but which, along with the occasional monument and statue, embodied the one emotion that Americans do better than anyone else — civic pride. Crucially, the open countryside could be seen from any high vantage point: this was not an environment that turned its back on the natural world and the human activities associated with it.

It was home to Morse's parents who were both educational psychologists by profession. What musical influence there was, came from his mother, who played classical piano — by all accounts to a reasonable standard, although Morse would later state that his parents were not particularly interested in music. Presbyterian by religion, his father was a spare-time minister, which meant that, as Morse revealed in a 2014 interview, 'For a number of years we didn't have any pop music or radio music in the house unless it was very mellow. So, I guess the next thing I remember was Harry Belefonte.'[9]

Morse has said that he avoided the prohibition by listening to pop music on a transistor radio smuggled into his bed.[10] His first instrument was the clarinet, which he took up because his brother David had already done so.

Morse's upbringing could hardly have been more middle class, even conventional. Family moves to Tennessee and Ypsilanti, Michigan, did not seriously disrupt the all-American idyll. But already an individualistic streak was beginning to make itself felt in Steve. He became increasingly dissatisfied with the clarinet because, as he said, it was too limited: it could play the melody in an ensemble piece and that was about it. He wanted something that would allow him to express his more creative ideas. It came in the form of what would become his signature instrument — the guitar.

The first time that he encountered one was at a local county fair. As he reported it: 'There was a guy working one of the booths, sitting behind it. I just snuck in between the booths and watched him just from a foot away. He was finger picking [a simple Dixie melody]; just a simple thing like that. I thought that was the coolest thing in the world. I was blown away that the guitar could make music.'[11] This tale has something of the 'pre-title sequence' about it but serves well to illustrate the milieu from which Morse came.

Another spark to his imagination was The Beatles (it is to be wondered how many thousands of times that sentence has been written in relation to some musician or other). His father's stern attitude to lowbrow culture notwithstanding, the young Steve was able to acquaint himself with the Fab Four's output and was frankly amazed at what he was hearing. He was impressed above all by the rhythms, 'Lennon's rhythm is so incredibility consistent, and George Harrison's little lead flourishes were just perfectly musical. And between those two, they were both playing the same instrument. And I felt this is great.'[12]

On the classical side, Bach was a major inspiration, an early indicator of the eclecticism that would go on to become a defining feature of Morse's own music.

His first guitar lesson was, according to him, somewhat

chaotic. Taking along a broken instrument found, possibly, by his grandmother in her attic, the only thing he learned was that it was unplayable. The remedy was for him to rent an acoustic Gibson for five dollars a month. It saw him through the first year or so of his training. As he has said, though, try as he might, he could not make it sound like The Beatles — or Bach. Nonetheless, after only a couple of days he was playing songs (the old school kid stalwart 'House Of The Rising Sun' was probably the first that he learned).

His progress being good, he acquired a guitar of his own, a Music Master. He played it through a mono-record player amp cobbled together by his father. In not much more time, he began to outpace his instructor, whose approach of transcribing songs from the radio was by its nature insufficiently creative for Morse.

An early manifestation of his desire to break bounds was his formation of a band with his brother Dave, which went under the not especially enticing name of The Plague. Quite what their music was like is hard to ascertain: obviously, there are no extant recordings of it, but, since the band consisted of three guitars plugged into one amp and a bass amp that needed the occasional kick to keep it going, it was probably not an overly sophisticated sound.

It is not certain what appeared on The Plague's average set list, but whatever it was, it was not original. The band played at high school dances and the like. Regardless of its merits as art, the experience was another piece in the jigsaw puzzle of Morse's life, or, to follow a metaphor that we have been using, another line on the flight plan. It proved to be a vital one. It was while doing this that Morse chose his path: 'I played in my brother's band,' he has said, 'and at some point, as a teenager I got really serious, more into the soloing, and realised I was going to do it for the rest of my life.'[13]

That epiphany having been achieved; it was about to be overtaken by a more important event. The boys' father was given a job at the Medical College of Georgia, which meant that the family upped sticks again, this time heading to Augusta.

This was a huge change. Morse was going to live in the South and, in this context, that is more than just a geographical term. The differences between America's Northern and Southern states go back to the days known as the 'antebellum' period.[14]

The North is, in many ways, a continuation of — perhaps perfection of — the Old Europe that begat it. It is industrialised, progressive and business orientated. All Ivy League Universities are in the North, as are many of the states that dependably vote Democrat. It is multi-cultural, for certain, but its architectural vernacular is the stone-clad skyscraper, which we might imagine is what the masons who built Medieval cathedrals would be working on were they still alive today.

A large chunk of the North is called New England for a reason. It is also, it must be said, the part of the country in which slavery never took root. Indeed, it was the issue of whether forcing people to work without pay should continue to be legal that largely brought about the nineteenth century cataclysm from the ashes of which was born modern America.

The South, by contrast, has always been seen as more conservative, if not politically (although, yes okay, politically), then morally. Religion, specifically protestant Christianity, is all powerful. Ideas about what constitutes 'proper' behaviour follow from it. Morse became starkly aware of this from the moment of his arrival: 'As soon as we stepped off the plane and said, "Hello, Georgia," rednecks started hassling me and my brother — immediately. Because our hair was halfway over our ears, and it was totally unheard of.'[15] This was followed up by his being jumped by a gang of thugs the next day with the consequence that his arrival at his new school was marred by his face being covered with bruises. The hair problem was not to be resolved for some time.

Economically, Southern states have tended to be rural in character and agricultural. They have therefore been poorer than their Northern neighbours and, as the young Morse found to his cost, slower to adopt the trappings and mores of modernity. Sometimes, this goes back to ownership of the plantations on which slaves of African origin were put to work picking cotton and tobacco. The process of bringing an end to such places cost more American lives than any other conflict ever, including the World Wars. The process was not quite complete even as Morse's family was moving there, the civil rights movement still being very active.

The newly arrived Morse, then, stood out both as a person and for what he represented. As he put it, 'I had a big culture shock going from the North to the South. And, you know, at the age of 12 and a half — going from having all of your friends to suddenly being a stranger and a Yankee to boot.'[16]

He was different from his new classmates in many ways. His predecessors had been on one side of the Civil War, theirs the other. He spoke one way, they another.

Of course, none of this should be overplayed. *The Simpsons* may have poked fun at the people of Dixieland in the hick shitkicker form of Cletus the Slack-Jawed yokel, but he is something of a stereotype. The South can boast an intellectual tradition to rival that of the North and it should not be forgotten that many distinctively American musical styles and genres originated there, often in the crucible of its black community. Blues, jazz and gospel can all be mentioned in this connection, while country music, probably the ultimate sound of America, is regarded by many Southerners as an alternative, or side, religion.

Morse continued to rub up against his new surroundings while at Richmond Academy, his high school. Surprisingly for anyone who has met the adult version, he was viewed as a troublemaker. It was all about that pesky hair. The school superintendent would visit every two weeks and would dependably send Morse away, telling him that he had to get his hair cut. Morse's response was to remove the absolute bare minimum that he could get away with. It did little good. In his final year, the principal threatened to withhold his report card unless he fell into line. Musically, this period was catastrophic because it caused Morse to give up playing altogether, mainly for lack of access to possible band mates.

One eventually came along and revivified him. His name was Allen: he was a fellow Northerner, but his chief attraction was that he owned an amp. Morse has described him as having a hippy mentality. He and Morse would spend hours in each other's bedrooms listening to records and playing along to them. Morse has said: 'That helped our music because there was no social life whatsoever except being underground in that kind of an environment.'[17] They started to play together at a local coffeehouse that, in a nice piece of Beatles synchronicity, was called the Glass Onion.

At around the same time, Morse formed one of his most important and enduring relationships. While in the tenth grade, he met Andy West, a figure who was to weave in and out of his story for as long as there was a story. The chief bond between the two was, naturally, music. West has spoken of how he, a developing bass player, was made aware of Morse, who was already gaining a reputation as a 'hot shot guitar player.' He introduced himself, only then realising that he and Morse were in the same school. This earned West an invitation to come and jam with Morse's band and generally hang out. Thus, a lifelong friendship was formed.

West has credited Morse with helping to improve his playing: 'I definitely give that credit to him. Steve was a great friend to me and I've loved doing it but I didn't really know that much about music, per se. I never really became a good journeyman musician. You know, someone who has studied all the greats and figured out how all this stuff works.'[18]

Seeing potential in each other, the two formed a group called Three, which played a twenty-minute set consisting of pieces by Beethoven, 'Greensleeves' and instrumental versions of songs by Cream and others.

This soon morphed into Dixie Grit, with Dave Morse as drummer, Johnny Carr on keyboards and Frank Brittingham on guitar and vocals. Minor local successes, they played together for a year or so before the enterprise fizzled out and everyone, or nearly everyone, went their separate ways. Dave dropped out of music, other than it being a pastime, to become an academic.

As musical seeds were being planted though, the hair situation refused to resolve itself. It became so bad that two things happened: firstly, Morse was 'rezoned' into a different school and, secondly, he bought a short hair wig. The latter came about as a result of his talking to Army Reservists from nearby Fort Gordon who attended the gigs that he was playing in the local area. They taught him how to hide long hair in order to sidestep overly strict regulations.

Although Morse's new principal was relatively sympathetic to the fashions of the young, the dreaded superintendent still required a visit to the barber. At first, the wig ruse worked beautifully in mollifying the persecutors, even if it did cause Morse to look a little strange.

Unfortunately, the local Board of Education got wise to what was going on and banned wigs. Morse was called to the principal's office and told to lose his. Not wanting to antagonise a man who he saw as reasonably sound, he agreed, but joined a march of students against the rather draconian anti-long hair rules.

In an age of agitation for greater freedoms, the event excited some interest in the media and Morse made what was probably his first TV appearance when he told a reporter: 'The Board of Education has no interest in education. I've got one of the highest grade averages in the school, maybe in the county, I don't know. But I'm being kicked out of school because they just knew that I just wasn't exactly the same underneath the short-haired wig.'[19]

It was only at this point that his parents found out. They asked him what he was planning to do. Being by now sixteen, he decided to drop out of school altogether and get on with his life. They were naturally mortified; as he had told that reporter, he was far from a poor student. Quite the contrary.

He had friends at a local school called Aquinas, but there were problems with his joining them. As its name implied, it was denominationally Catholic. Indeed, it was run by nuns. It was also private. The first of these was solved uncontroversially. As Morse has said, he was used to religion and the tenets of Catholicism were not that novel to him; everyone worshipped the same God. The second was taken care of by his agreeing to work off the cost of tuition should his parents be prepared to advance it to him. They were. From Morse's perspective, the best thing about the school was that it only insisted on a shirt and tie; hair could be any length.

Having found an accepting environment, Morse thrived. He carried on playing gigs and excelled at his schoolwork. Completing Grade 11, he was placed on a programme for early access to college. Higher education only took him to the next state along from Georgia, one which, despite being technically further south, is not generally considered to be of the South: Florida.

He was inspired to apply to the University of Miami having heard the Cuban guitarist Juan Mercadal at a concert sponsored by the Classical Guitar Society of Georgia. As Morse put it, 'He was playing classical guitar with a lot of energy... I was a teenager and teenagers will — you know how they are. It was very energetic and for a teenage kid who was playing Led Zeppelin, I could just see it. I said, "Wow! Wouldn't it be great if I could do that too? Then I could be a real guitar player!" That's what it was. It was that simple.'[20]

Mercadal was a tutor at the University, teaching a class in Classical Guitar. Eventually, he took on Morse as a pupil, but only after Morse had ceased to be the kind of 'beginner' that he tended to ignore.

Thanks to that concert, Morse was on his way out of the South.

He was able to transfer to the University of Miami early because it was a private institution. But he needed to prove his musicianship, so, as he said, 'The next thing I needed was an audition tape with me playing classical guitar. So, I got a classical guitar and this book that says, "You Too Can Play the Classical Guitar", and I learned a piece from it.'[21] Unable at that point to read music, he mastered a Bach piece note-for-note, a process that took some time.

Soon enough, Andy West joined him, following a tortuous route that caused him to be a year behind Morse in college, having been a year ahead at school. It did not matter. Take off had been achieved: the flight of Morse's life was on its way to reaching cruising altitude, but not without first hitting plenty of turbulence.

2.
Name Dropping

Attending university immediately set Morse apart from many of those with whom he would go on to share stages and pages in the future. While popular musicians have never been completely averse to learning their craft the hard way, their conventional approach has tended to be much more informal.[22]

They prioritise self-expression and emotion over technical accuracy. Much of their learning is done, so to speak, on-the-job, by picking up an instrument and trying to get some kind of pleasant sound out of it. The likes of Pete Hook, the bassist from New Order, have spoken about how ignorance even of which strings on a guitar correlate to which notes is not necessarily a barrier to writing a chart-busting tune.[23]

Related, but not identical, is the fact that rock has traditionally not been a middle-class art form — from both the perspective of its creation and its consumption.[24]

With its roots in various folk styles, it has more readily been seen as the soundtrack of the blue-collar world, failing to achieve the seal of bourgeois approval that has attached itself to, say, jazz. The closest it has got to such lofty heights has been its growing acceptance by 'nerds' and 'geeks', who have used it as an outlet for emotions that might otherwise remain defiantly 'pent up.'[25]

The upshot is that, for someone from Morse's background, taking up rock music might, in a different age, have been vilified as patronising, or tacitly celebrated as ironic.

But Miami University Music School was, in the early 1970s, in the vanguard of a more enlightened way of thinking. Under its Dean, William F. Lee, it introduced programmes in all manner of genres and practices — including Music Engineering Technology — that would have been anathema at many a more traditional institution.

Consequently, Morse's circle included not only Andy West, but pioneers such as Jaco Pastorius and Pat Metheny. Of his student days, Morse has said, 'You come from a small town like I did and these new guys are in the class: Pat? Metheny? Nice to meet you! Well, let's play. He could hear anything I played and he could respond to it. He had the ear and when it came to the jazz stuff — and I was not a jazz guy — that was his other jamming that he did with people.'[26]

Metheny was so adept that the University had him teach lessons, despite his being a student; as Morse has said, when someone is that good, what exactly can he learn from anyone else? He led classes in electric guitar, the introduction of which was typical of the University's forward-thinking approach.

With Pastorius, who taught bass, jamming proved to be especially fruitful for Morse. It took place in Pastorius' apartment, which was in Lauderdale. Morse has said that his car barely made it out that far and he went inside to find the place a mess. Somewhat eccentric in his approach, Pastorius insisted that no music could be made until all present had jogged along the beach a few times, running on sand being tough even for the fit youth that Morse was at the time.

Suitably energised, Morse expected that the jam could start, but no: it had to wait again until a little body surfing had been completed. Such rituals aside, the influence was inspirational. Morse has spoken about how he could hardly believe how many notes Pastorius was capable of squeezing into a short space of time: surely, he thought, such speed must cause some sort of physical injury. Morse saw Pastorius play gigs in the local area, producing 'superfast two finger stuff' that added up to a unique sound.

Considering this period and the golden circle of musicians with whom Morse passed it with, Metheny in particular stands out. He was a catalyst for so much that happened — and not just for Morse. Take another contemporary, one who needs little introduction, Hiram Bullock.

He would go on to have a wonderful career, working alongside all manner of greats. With Morse, he played bass in the brief period before Andy West enrolled in the school. He was laid back about the repertoire with which he was presented and, again, skilled enough to take on whatever was thrown his way. But his recollections focus on much the same things as Morse's: 'I studied with Pat Metheny. He had a very different sound in those days. He was a guy who had a very clear idea of what he wanted to do at an early age. To me, it was almost intimidating how mature he was.'[27] It should be clear that the free form jamming that Morse undertook with Metheny was absolutely central to his development.

Equally beneficial was his playing in bands for musical theatre productions. It was, perhaps inevitably, Metheny who recommended that Morse replace him in the pit at Miami's Coconut Grove Playhouse while he was away touring. 'That is a great experience, too,' Morse has said, 'Seeing all the people backstage, talking to them, seeing the trials and tribulations of the whole thing, from the backstage to looking at it from the front. That's really good experience for anybody. I think everybody needs to know the humanity of what's involved when you do a show.'[28] His eyes were opened to the sheer complexity of a full performance, despite it only being those on stage who get the applause.

It was what Morse has characterised as a 'reading gig,' as it involved sight-reading and playing from scratch (learning to read music had been his highest priority upon enrolling at college). Many of the scores had been written by pianists and so were not as helpful as they could have been for string players — again there was a need for in-the-moment creativity on his part. An example was a show for which he was required to play banjo, an instrument with which he was not overly familiar. His solution was to buy a banjo and tune it like a guitar, although, as he has said, since the parts were in E-flat, it would have sounded the same however he had done it.

Another epiphany came when Morse discovered the jazz fusion guitarist John McLaughlin, leader of the Mahavishnu Orchestra. This seems to have been one of the many happy accidents that pepper this story. McLaughlin was playing a gig at the University that was supposed to take place outside, but it had to be moved into the canteen due to inclement weather. Morse just happened to be buying a peanut butter sandwich for lunch as it was being set up and he positioned himself right next to the stack of Marshall amps in order to get both the best sound and the best view. McLaughlin's picking style helped to crystallise Morse's study of Jimmy Page's similar work with Led Zeppelin in pushing his playing to a whole new level.

What this all added up to was an education in open-mindedness and musical fusion. It entered the melting pot of influences that

Morse was already quietly stirring. Prior to entering the University, Morse had seen gigs by Hendrix, Janis Joplin and Dave Brubeck among others. All were important for him. They were added to some artists already mentioned — The Beatles, The Rolling Stones, The Yardbirds — in shaping his thinking. The preponderance of British guitarists is intriguing and ultimately significant (it is easily forgotten that Hendrix, despite being American, was 'discovered' by the British). Morse practised by rehearsing their songs. One cover version that Morse performed with his brother after school one day was that of a track that had fairly recently been a big hit in America — 'Hush' by an up-and-coming British act called Deep Purple.

Perhaps Miami's most powerful long-term impact on Morse was this willingness to experiment and bring different styles together. The people that he met, many of whom were fellow students, amounted to an informal faculty for him. Many would go on to become his professional colleagues. Some fell by the wayside; Bullock's take was, 'I'm not a big one for fusion, you know... To me, fusion always implied more power rock elements, like Chick Corea's electric bands. That's the closest to what I think of as fusion: odd time signatures and real powerful, loud, virtuosic playing.'[29]

Bullock's words were, it might be conceded, confirmed by Morse's student group, which put its genre into its name, Rock Ensemble 2. This came about as a reaction against jazz, as Morse has said: 'There was one rock ensemble that played sort of jazz-rock, which was mostly jazz. So, I said, "Let me do another one, and it will be more of a rock ensemble." [The faculty] said, "Okay," so it was Rock Ensemble No. 2.'[30]

As lacking in creativity as the name seems to be, it was only ever provisional: Morse always referred to the band as Dixie Dregs. Dixie Grit may have split up, but Morse and West had not been so ready to give up on the project. As the former said, 'Andy and I were keen to keep on playing instrumental music on our own. So, since we were the only ones left from the group, or the dregs of the group, we called it Dixie Dregs.'[31]

This story is intriguing in debunking the notion that the name was intended to be a reference to the type of unsavoury people who can be denoted by the word 'dregs.' Irrespective of its origins, it would echo down the decades, turning into a central element in Morse's musical identity. But that was for the future. For now, it was part of its members' studies, Morse officially being 'instructor'. Alongside him were West on bass, Burt Yarnald on drums, Frank Josephs on keyboards and the violinist Allen Sloan.

In a callback to his school days, Morse's sense of style was perhaps the most attention-grabbing thing about the band. His home-assembled guitar excited particular interest. With a telecaster body, a Stratocaster neck and a Gibson bridge, it became informally known as the 'Frankenstein Telecaster' and achieved something of a following in its own right. Rod Morgenstein, fellow student and, later, a Dreg himself, said of Morse at this stage in his life: 'He would change pickups as he was soloing and his lines didn't sound like stock bebop lines. But his teacher kept asking him, "Why can't you sound like this guy?" Steve was just doing his own thing.'[32]

It was a familiar struggle with authority that became milder as Morse became more practised. By his senior recital — effectively an examination — he felt comfortable enough to deliver a performance consisting of original compositions for classical guitar followed by the Ensemble playing a short set — which flew in the face of the usual requirement for jazz covers.

More widely, the band followed the usual pattern of gigging around the University and at small venues in Miami, their repertoire — presaging things to come — consisting largely of instrumentals written by Morse, with a few covers of tunes by the Allman Brothers' and the Mahavishnu Orchestra to bulk out the running time.

They began to build something of an underground fan base. 'When we first started it was pretty much me calling bars and saying, "Can we come and play?"' West has said, 'For us, it was winning the audience over and until we had a full canon of Steve's music that we could play, we were playing whatever we knew how to play. It was drawn from rock traditions — Zeppelin, Allman Brothers, you know — until we got heavily into the Mahavishnu thing which then you know my other sound bite is we were like a Mahavishnu Orchestra cover band, which is bizarre.'[33]

Important insights were gained at this time which influenced how they operated in later years, 'We learned that it was really about the energy of the music and how people respond to it.' West added, 'So we learned how to engender ourselves to an audience where they would like what we did. And so, it wasn't always about, "Oh you know here's some stuff you'll never understand but we're going to play it anyways." It wasn't like that.'[34]

Their ambitions did not stop there, however, and Morse's first ever recorded material was produced in a concert hall on campus. Morse described the process: 'The recording itself was stark and unpolished. We had to record it in one night after a long day of school and classes. It was done late at night. We were 19–20-year-olds. It wasn't really a studio. They just put the recording equipment in a live concert hall. We were set up in there with headphones. My amp was in an elevator shaft. The violin, Fender Rhodes and bass went direct. The drums were on stage. It was bizarre.'[35] The line-up was that of Rock Ensemble 2, with Morgenstein coming in for Yarnald, who had injured himself while surfing. The result was a short album that went under the title, *The Great Spectacular.*

Morse's critique of its sound cannot really be put to the test because, in its original form, it is no longer available. Supposedly, most of the vinyl-only copies melted in a truck as they were being transported north during one of the band's tours. Barely enough survived to be used as demos to send out to record companies. More positively, most of the tracks were subsequently re-recorded for inclusion on 'official' Dixie Dregs releases.

Listening to them now, the main surprise is how fully formed they sound. There is little to distinguish them in terms of style and slickness from the likes of 'Take It Off The Top.' 'Refried Funky Chicken,' for example, is as whacky as its title suggests, incorporating a funkier-than-thou bass line, numerous stops and starts and a violin solo that would grace any bluegrass-inflected hoe down.

Morse's spot, when it comes, consists of the kind of wailing guitar that might better suit a genuine rock ensemble. By contrast, 'Wages Of Weirdness' is surprisingly non-weird, although it is another funk fest. 'The Great Spectacular' itself is rocky in places, but flirts here and there with folk. It does demonstrate Morse's ability to write the kind of riffs that sound like they were intended to accompany films of sports cars eating up the miles in some picturesque country setting.

The key word, again, is 'fusion.' The chief impression that these tracks give of Morse the composer is of someone with a restless imagination who is not content to stick to one style, one structure, one mood. They jump around, alight on a tune, or riff, or tempo, only to discard it seconds later in favour of a new thing. They are instrumentals by default: they simply do not have the through line, the rigidity, the — it might as well be said — discipline required for a singer to write verses and choruses over the top of them.

Are they entertaining? They are certainly very well played, but whether you enjoy them will depend on your capacity to be surprised by music. They will appeal if you find delight in the unpredictable. If you are someone who likes to dance to music, you will be lost — they do not have the repetitive qualities needed for that.

Anyway, they achieved what they were designed to achieve, because they were part of the mix that led to Steve Morse and the Dixie Dregs being signed by a record label, a proper record label. An outcome that, for Morse at least, had always seemed to be on the cards, was about to occur.

3.
Out Standing In Their Field

In 1976, two things happened that are worth reporting. The first was that Morse, through being in a particular place at a particular time, played on the Liza Minnelli album *Tropical Nights* (released in 1977). Apparently, he was in a studio and Minelli's band was in the one next door looking for someone to supply a country-style guitar line for the song 'When It Comes Down to It.' Mistaking Morse for a random redneck and therefore versed in the required genre, they approached him and, having nothing better to do, he obliged. He has never heard the completed track. Or met Liza Minelli, who was not present that day.

More significant developments occurred around Christmas, when the Dregs were performing at a club in Nashville called the Exit Inn. Its location should say everything about the type of music that patrons expected — and wanted. But Morse and his colleagues were giving them the strange hybrid of rock, bluegrass and the Mahavishnu Orchestra that was their stock in trade. How well it went down has not been recorded, but history has noted that there happened to be a famous musician sitting at the bar — none other than Chuck Leavell, piano player with — you couldn't make this up — the Allman Brothers. Rod Morgenstein has spoken about how, one by one, the members of the band spotted him. His presence galvanised them and they put everything they could into the show.

Afterwards, Leavell went up to them and, as Morgenstein reports it, 'He said, "Who are you guys and where can I buy your records? I'm on tour with the Allman Brothers; we had a night off and I thought I would come in, have a beer and see some local country band and I'm seeing this instrumental fusion, you know, Mahavishnu Orchestra kind of group." Whatever. It's because of him that we got our first record deal because, true to his word, the next day he called Phil

Walden, who was the president of Capricorn Records, told hm about the band he had seen the night before and said, "You have to sign them."'[36]

That, at least, is one version of the story and, since it comes from Morgenstein, there is no reason to disbelieve it. Another — Morse's, as it happens — is more nuanced. 'The Allman Brothers had broken up,' he said, 'and Chuck Leavell started Sea Level. They were just doing small gigs, trying to get tight. And we got on a gig in Nashville, and we had a little following there. So, we opened the gig with them and freaked out Chuck and Twiggs [Lyndon]. Twiggs was there looking for a gig.'[37]

Sea Level were an offshoot of the Allman Brothers (the band's name was a pun on Leavell's: 'C. Leavell'). Twiggs Lyndon had been the Allman Brothers' roadie and, as such, had become well known in his own right. According to Morse, Lyndon was the main attraction because the Dregs wanted to use him but were unable to match his usual rate. Fortunately, his enthusiasm for their music led to his offering to work for whatever they could afford (West remembers this as happening later during a gig at a place called Rosa's Cantina — a name that Morse would bring back over twenty years later when writing for Deep Purple).

Anyway, it seems that Lyndon's offer, rather than anything that Leavell did, was the spur for what happened next. On this telling, Leavell, Lyndon and someone from BMI who had been at the Exit Inn gig called Walden the next day simply to say, 'have a listen to this band,' there not being any overt push for them to be offered a contract. Morgenstein's fairy tale telling leaves out another crucial detail: the Dregs had been doing everything they could to get Walden's attention for a while.

Where the two accounts agree is on how Walden heard them play: a personal audition in Capricorn Records' hometown of Macon, Georgia. According to Morgenstein, it took place at a club and Walden brought everyone from the label, up to and including the office cat. Leavell was present and took the stage to jam on a run through of the Allman Brothers' 'Jessica' (now better known, at least to those resident in the UK, as the theme tune to the motoring magazine TV show *Top Gear*).

The ensuing contract took some time to ratify, a period during which the band members were obliged to remain quiet both for legal reasons and to avoid jinxing the deal. When they finally got into a studio, it was to create an album that West for one considers to be their first 'proper' output, *The Great Spectacular* being relegated to demo status. The line-up was unchanged from the one that had so impressed Leavell and Lyndon, apart from Steve Davidowski coming in on keyboards. This addition came about because he happened to be in Augusta — to which most of the Dregs, including Morse, had decamped after college, living frugally in property rented to them by West's parents.

Experimentation was the main theme of the recording process. Attempting to create a 'total rhythm section,' all five members played together, most going direct to the mixers with Morse's amp muffled. The result was an unsatisfactory sound that necessitated later redubs to cover the moments that were particularly unlistenable.

At the suggestion of the producer, Stuart Levine, backward tracked guitar was featured, the aim being to play melodies, rather than the solos that were the usual way in which the technique was used. All tracks were Morse compositions and all were instrumentals. Three were remakes from *The Great Spectacular.*

The recording process was one that the perfectionist Morse did not enjoy as much as playing live. The studio was cold and because he was there all the time, he was conscious of every little wrong note or variation from a track as written. As he has said, when listening to a band playing live, mistakes are either missed or mentally edited out by the audience, but playing in a studio, when only one instrument is coming through a pair of headphones, poor tuning will be very obvious — and getting in tune with little time and a low temperature was no easy feat.

The result of it all, *Free Fall*, released on May 27th, 1977, is a 'here we are, notice us' piece of work. The eclecticism that the band had become known for is very much present, but the style is recognisably their own. Bluegrass is prominent in 'Moe Down,' some rather sophisticated jazz in 'Cosmopolitan Traveller,' bluesy Hammond organ is all over the place, but, for the most part, the album is funky. The bass bounces around while Morse brings in screaming guitars and a few groovy riffs.

'Cruise Control,' a track to which the band would return, is perhaps the most typical, a laid-back collection of solos by all the instruments over a bass line and drum beat that just won't quit.

Quieter moments, especially those that showcase the violin, are among the album's highlights. Overall, it undoubtedly demonstrates the virtuosity of the players, but the feel is closer to easy listening than the punk rock that was redefining pop music at the time of its release.

It is musically complex, for sure, and has aged well in terms of its entertainment value but coming from someone — Morse — who had spent much of his life defying authority, it is rather conventional. It plays with different genres but does not do much to challenge or change them. It also does not fit too readily into Capricorn's house style, which was a type of southern boogie; indeed, at the time, the label was a major centre for music of that type. Jazzy, funky fusion music was not really what they were about.

The album managed a modest commercial performance and reviewers were kind to it. In its support, the band continued to play relatively unambitious venues, such as the Tennessee State Fairgrounds on 26th September and Peacock Park, Miami, on 3rd October.[38] To help with costs, Lyndon built the 'Black Hearted Woman,' which was a trailer converted into a makeshift tour bus with six (probably less than luxurious) bunk beds. There was no door: to gain entry, band members had to slide in through a hole at window height.

On the tour, some nights were more successful than others. A free gig in Montgomery, Alabama, for which the Dregs were part of a larger bill, descended into ugly violence as bottle-throwing troublemakers were confronted by irate members of the crowd who were there for the music. Only the intervention of the local police quietened things down in time for Morse and his colleagues to take the stage.

On another occasion, they found themselves playing at a social evening for the parents and pupils of Virginia Military Academy. This audience was expecting nothing more than a little light background music while they chatted and drank their sodas. Unsurprisingly, they were so befuddled by the noise to which they were subjected that they begged the band to stop (the whole incident surely inspired a very similar scene in the classic film *This Is Spinal Tap*). Finding Dregs' set lists from this time is difficult, but new pieces were certainly given a live airing, 'Cruise Control' and 'Freefall' being examples.

A second album followed in quick succession. Given that no one in the band had been too enamoured of the sound of *Free Fall*, it was perhaps inevitable that there would be changes for its follow-up. Davidowski was out. This was not completely surprising: he seems to have not fully engaged with the band's style from his first rehearsal with them — which did not go well: 'I was using a little suitcase piano and these guys had amps running up all along the wall. As soon as they hit the first note, I jumped up and it actually made me mad. I got up and said, "I can't do this!"'[39]

He toured diligently for a while, but not always enthusiastically — he described a date at New York's CBGB club as a 'mis-booking'[40] although that was probably fair enough. Thus, when presented with an offer to return to his preferred jazz, Davidowski took it with alacrity. In his place was installed Mark Parrish, who had been associated with the band since their Dixie Grit days.

The other change in personnel was arguably more crucial. Gone was Levine, to be replaced by Ken Scott. This was something of a coup for the band. As West has said, 'We'd always wanted to work with [Scott] because he'd engineered for the Mahavishnu Orchestra, one of our heroes.'[41]

Morse added more detail: 'Somehow luck had it that he finally heard some of the stuff we'd sent him, or something like that. All of a sudden, we found out we could do an album with Ken Scott — if we went in the studio the next week, or something ridiculous like that.'[42]

Scott brought a new methodology: over-record if necessary, so that everything on the album sounds as good as it can be. The rhythm section was laid down first and other instruments were layered on top of it, although difficulties with the pitching of the bass meant that overdubs were necessary, causing the budget — more generous than on the first album — to become strained.

Still, the album that emerged, *What If*, is one of the highlights of the band's career. It is unusual in not consisting exclusively of Morse's compositions. 'Travel Tunes' is credited to West alone. He described how it came about: 'That came out of that four-track recorder era. Steve brought the guitar lines and chordal patterns, but I'd otherwise written and recorded the melodies and the form.'[43] On another. 'Gina Lola Breakdown' Morse shares the writing with Twiggs Lyndon.

'Take It Off The Top' gets things off to a spirited start, to be followed by 'Odyssey,' a long, stylistically complicated piece that flirts with dissonance while recalling country and folk. The meditative, almost classical title track is next. Side two brings back the funk for 'Ice Cakes,' before showcasing Morse's acoustic skills in the lovely, minimalist 'Little Kids.' 'Night Meets Light' brings proceedings to a close.

Overall, it is less obviously funky than its predecessor — and probably more accessible to the casual listener. Released in March 1978, it was another commercial belly flop, as much as critics praised it. On the plus side, it did score the band a slot supporting Santana at a gig at the Fox Theatre in Atlanta on 24th March.

Writing for the *Atlanta Journal and Constitution*, Bill King was full of praise: 'If you prefer music that leans heavily toward the instrumental side... then you really missed a treat. While the Dixie Dregs, who opened the show, are a relatively young group, they more than held their own against Santana. The group's unique fusion of jazz, rock, country and classical was enthusiastically received by the Atlanta crowd. Especially impressive were guitarist Steve Morse and electric violinist Allen Sloan. Morse's soaring guitar solos and Sloan's versatility on violin — ranging from country fiddle to classical — blended extremely well. Not only was the Dregs' music infectiously happy, the band members themselves seemed to be greatly enjoying the performance. The multi-faceted rendition of the song "Cruise Control" brought the Fox audience to its feet, demanding an encore. Hopefully we can look forward to seeing this group returning to the Fox as headliners in the not-too-distant future.'

What If also achieved a reasonable amount of traction in Europe. As a result, an invitation came in to play at the Montreux Jazz Festival on 23rd July.

Morse has suggested that this happened because the legendary Claude Nobs — the festival's curator — had an ear for unusual and 'weird' music and liked what he heard enough to get the Dregs on to the ticket when Capricorn called pushing for another of their acts, Sea Level to appear. To some extent, another portent of things to come, the festival was the latest of many occasions on which the sheer musicality of the band was the main theme.

Released as a concert album years after the event, it has also been preserved as a film. Both highlight how incredibly tight the band were in performance, so tight, in fact, that some of the songs were used in these recordings on their next 'studio' album.

Hence, several 'new' tracks are featured, including 'Night Of The Living Dregs' and 'The Bash.' The former is a laid-back chunk of funk, energised by some heavy fuzz guitar chords and furious violin soloing. The latter, a country piece so American it practically smells of apple pie, is considered by many to be the standout, the presence of 'Take It Off The Top' notwithstanding. Its composition is credited to the whole band, suggesting that it may have had its origins in a jam.

West's take was, 'By the time we got to Montreux, we'd toured a lot playing those songs. We'd crafted sets to win over an audience, and the audience there definitely didn't know what to expect from us at first. But they increasingly got into it. It was the right moment in time for us.'[44]

That the concert happened at all is testament to the band's — and Morse's — growing stature, artistically, if not commercially. Morse does not hog the limelight. On the film, he often seems a little bashful, allowing others, particularly Sloan, to do the showboating. That is not to say that he is not completely at home on the stage; he has spoken about the difference between studio recording and live playing, resoundingly preferring the latter, 'It's not as spontaneous or natural — that's the main thing that impresses me about the studio. You can get great sounds, but it's harder to play in the studio.'[45]

Another major moment for the band came almost exactly a year later when they finally made it to the West Coast and played the Roxy in LA. The gig was attended by a number of celebrities, although the precise list is one of those that changes depending on who tells the story. Billy Cobham — together with his band — and fusion legend Stanley Clarke were certainly there. Jeff Beck may or may not have been. Either way, it was a big moment for the band in terms of recognition.

But, in showbiz, moments of glory are always followed by a return to the more workaday and mundane. Outside of these high points, the Dregs were still playing such inauspicious venues as varsity gymnasiums in North Carolina. Important steps had, however, been taken. If nothing else, the band had already recorded some of the pieces for their next album.

That album, *Night Of The Living Dregs*, was released in April

1979. Again, produced by Ken Scott, it is a thing of two halves. The first side consists of new studio tracks, while the second half gathers the Montreux material — the two tracks already mentioned, together with, 'Leprechaun Promenade' and 'Patchwork.' The studio side begins with the fast-paced 'Punk Sandwich,' the title of which may be a nod to the genre that had been rewriting the rule book in recent years, despite the music itself sounding nothing like it. Then comes 'Country House Shuffle,' 'The Riff Raff' and 'Long Slow Distance.' All are what might be expected: stylistically diverse, hard-to-pigeonhole, but played with great aplomb and brio.

The album received typically positive reviews: The *Montreal Star* said of it, 'This latest outing catches the Dregs first in the studio and then in live performance on Side Two. Improvised music with grit.'[46]

Likewise gig reviews were also positive, even if the Dregs weren't drawing large crowds. Despite being a Saturday, a gig at the Macon City Auditorium on 13th October was played to an audience of only around 600.

David Bedingfield, writing for the *Macon Telegraph* put this down to the sophistication of the Dregs' music. In his review Bedingfield said, 'listening to the Dregs makes you feel like a 10th grader tackling James Joyce — you simply haven't yet acquired the equipment necessary to enjoy what's going on. The Dregs break all the rules. And to appreciate that, you first must know the rules that are being broken.'

Bedingfield continued his review by saying, 'too often, the Dregs race off and leave a befuddled audience way behind. That's not to say that's a terrible thing; indeed, many times in the midst of trying to find out just where the band is headed, you hear things you didn't think a guitar, keyboards, violin, bass, and drums were capable of producing.'

He continued: 'Many times the Dregs remind you of the smartest braggart in high school — forever trying to impress you with his virtuosity, successful only in driving you away. It's a little like listening to a teacher give you all the declensions of some obscure Latin noun. You're impressed he's able to do it, but it's not the sort of thing you want to spend your Saturday night listening to.'

'That sort of criticism, admittedly, bespeaks a lack of knowledge on the listener's part. If only the listener understood the language, then perhaps the manipulation of it in intricate contortions might make a more favourable impression.'

'What the Dregs want to do, it seems, is marry forms of music that seem at first listen to be wholly incompatible. The band is first and foremost a rock band. Steve Morse's screaming electric guitar, Andy West's booming bass, and Rod Morgenstein's pounding drums almost lock the group into the heavy backbeat of the rock and roll garage band.'

'These five musicians (Mark Parrish on keyboards and Allen Sloan on violin round out the group) are just so proficient that the music comes out — even to these untrained ears — sounding extraordinarily good.'

'But the marriage of rock and classical, or rock and country, or rock and jazz, doesn't always work. Sometimes the pounding of the guitars makes the songs sound like Keith Richards in a smack frenzy imitating riffs from a Bach concerto.'

'But then, if you venture out into uncharted regions, you're bound to step in a few potholes. This band manages to avoid the biggest — the one marked boredom — mainly with its uncommon bravery. One never knows where they're headed next. Steve Morse and Andy West play together on stage like they're reading each other's minds. They each seem to know what the other's doing about three minutes before we do. The grins on both their faces are not unlike those of two adolescents who have a secret they're slowly revealing — doing it bit by bit, impressing you with their knowledge, infuriating you with how complicated they're making the whole thing.'

Although Bedingfield was positive about the Dregs, perhaps reviews such as this were counter-productive and put your average rock fan off from investigating the band.

Night Of The Living Dregs shifted fewer copies than hoped for or expected. The band's members were not getting rich. Morse later remembered that 'We had three albums out and we were begging the record company to just guarantee us a hundred bucks a week. We figured a hundred bucks and we'd be set for life. On tour, we'd buy a couple of loaves of bread and some peanut butter. If we ever got to stay in a motel, we were really living. We had to all live together in a band house to pay the rent.'[47] In some ways though, that did not matter, because the band were about to become embroiled in the debacle that was the collapse of Capricorn Records.

The label had produced numerous hits over the years, but it, like many creative enterprises, had not consistently been able to generate sufficient revenue to guarantee longevity. In truth, the Allman Brothers had underwritten much of its activity and when they split up, the future looked bleak. Worse, the Brothers would go on to sue the label for unpaid royalties. Another contributing factor was Phil Walden himself: famously addicted to cocaine and booze, his behaviour was not that of a sober executive.

As Dick Woolley, Capricorn's vice president of promotions, put it: 'The price of success exacted an especially heavy toll on Phil... with the success of Capricorn his problems were raging out of his control; it manifested in embarrassing public tantrums that kept his lawyers busy putting out fires and it kept everyone in the office on edge. Phil's infamous temper outbursts were becoming more frequent and explosive; it was impossible to tell when something might set him off and when it did, friends and family alike made themselves scarce.'[48]

A proposed takeover by Warners got nowhere, although a distribution deal with PolyGram was more promising. It proved to be a double-edged sword: as sales declined, PolyGram tried to acquire the label themselves and, upon being rebuffed, demanded that Walden and his team hand over all assets, including the catalogue, as collateral on a five-million-dollar loan.

Most of Capricorn's artists, including the Dixie Dregs, left at this point. Walden did not take this well: 'They turned their back on me and started saying things that were not true. A lot of those people would still be playing Holiday Inns if it were not for Capricorn Records.'[49]

Morse claimed that he was unaware of any problems at the label: 'I was a fool because the only money you can get when you're in low record sales are the mechanical royalties for a writer. Those were due for three albums and they kept telling me about the computer which broke down. I should have smelled a rat.'[50]

Capricorn — and Walden — would rise again, but their involvement in this story is over for the time being. For the Dregs, and Steve Morse, it meant searching for a new home. Critical darlings — 'Night...' had scored a Grammy nomination for Best Rock Instrumental Performance — they had, as Morse hinted, yet to make a meaningful dent in the charts. Irrespective of that, Arista Records took them on and a new long player was recorded.

Line-up wise, it was all-change again as Parrish bowed out to be replaced with another old pal of the band's members in the form of (Terry) T. Lavitz. Thrift was the order of the day and so Morse not only wrote all of the music but produced. The result was *Dregs Of The Earth*, which was again adored by critics (albeit with the often-voiced caveat that the music was difficult to categorise), only to be largely ignored by the record-buying public.

That exclusively instrumental music was a hard sell could be one explanation for this, but Morse was less sure: 'Our problems have always been around people that say what's gonna be on the radio and people that say what's gonna get mass exposure.'[51] As much as lack of exposure was a problem, it did not stop the album from earning the band their second Grammy nomination.

Of *Dregs Of The Earth*, it can be said that it was another exercise in virtuosity that built on what had gone before, but without significantly developing it. This was most obvious in the track list including a re-recording of the track 'The Great Spectacular.' In one way, this was much needed in that the collapse of Capricorn meant that the band's previous releases were all now deleted and so nigh on impossible to find in shops. But it is still a re-recording.

The other tracks are the usual eclectic mix: 'Road Expense' is a welcome detour into rock, 'Broad Street Strut' a chance for Sloan to do his thing, 'Twiggs Approved' a bass-driven slice of heavy blues. The last of these, West has claimed, was inspired by Lyndon's taking upon himself the role of wise mentor, sharing with the band the benefit of his years of travelling the world with the Allman Brothers — what could and could not be loaded on trucks, for instance, or how sound systems needed to include some redundancy if they were to work with optimum efficiency.

The album is all entertaining and unquestionably the work of men who are consummately masters of their craft, but it is not really anything new. Perhaps it is a little heavier and rockier than the Dixie Dregs of old — and yet a piece of music that was already several years and several incarnations out of date still sounds perfectly at home. It was time to freshen things up. By changing, or rather dropping, a single word.

4.
Just Out Of Reach

What of Morse's private life? So far, a few of his relationships have been discussed, but they have all been with male friends and fellow professionals. Female readers might plausibly have reached this point wondering whether Morse ever even met a woman — apart from his mother — much less had anything to do with one. A particular woman will become highly significant towards the end of the story, but what of the early days?

Unfortunately, Morse comes across as essentially a shy man who says little about anything other than music — and few other people say much more about him than that either. He has never been a 'celebrity' as such: magazines have never paid to photograph his house, he has never featured in the gossip pages of newspapers, he has not developed into a social media 'influencer.' Finding information about him that is not directly related to his work as a musician is not easy — and probably unnecessary. After all, it is precisely a devotion to music that is his most salient characteristic.

Yet worries about money and providing for his family are a theme of most of his interviews from what could be called the First Dixie Dregs Era. By 1981, that family was in the process of being built, Morse having acquired a partner, Celeste, with whom he lived on a fifty-three-acre farm south of Augusta, near McDonough — a step up from the band houses of the past.

His passion for flying also took off (so to speak). He had been an aviation enthusiast all his life and had gained a pilot's licence in 1975 while working for a small delivery company. Now he had a turbo plane of his own and a makeshift runway on his property. In the future, flying would briefly become his main occupation, but it was useful even then, as Morse employed his skills to transport the band to venues for live performances. As extravagant as this sounds, it was actually another money-saving measure, since flying home after a concert meant that there was no need to pay for expensive hotels.

Morse was not the only member of his circle who regularly spent time in the air. Twiggs Lyndon was an accomplished sky diver who was in the habit of signalling the start of a Dregs gig by landing in front of the stage. He was indulging this interest on an otherwise unremarkable Friday in November 1979, having joined a formation team. Morse was a member of the watching crowd. Thanks to his parachute not opening, Lyndon plunged 12,000 feet to his death. According to the post-mortem, he suffered a heart attack on the way down. Morse, however, maintained that he likely froze due to his not wearing a properly insulated suit.

Lyndon had frequently spoken of suicide, but Morse dismissed the notion that what happened was deliberate, saying: 'He cut away [his parachute] and tried to go to his reserve chute, then tumbled with no signs of movement. I'm absolutely convinced that he lost consciousness due to shock and hypothermia. If Twiggs had wanted to kill himself, he would have gone out in style, freefalling into a target or something.'[52] When Lyndon's body was found, it was discovered that he had seemingly made no attempt to deploy the reserve chute. For Morse, the accident had led to the loss of both a colleague and a friend.

It was only one of many reasons why this was a tough time. Career matters were another: for all their skill and talent, the band was just not breaking through in any meaningful way. Morse intimated as much himself: 'I'm pretty dedicated to the cause. Things look pretty bad sometimes. Every once in a while, you'll be out in the middle of nowhere just realising it's gonna cost you money to play that night. You're gonna have to pay to play. And you go in the record store and the record's not there. It can just make you want to go to the bus stop and go home.'[53]

In accounting for the Dixie Dregs' somewhat niche appeal, the lack of vocals would be one culprit, eclecticism would be another. Being difficult to categorise can lend a certain excitement, but it can also cause confusion among potential listeners.

What sort of band were the Dixie Dregs trying to be? This appeared to be a question much posed at Arista Records who enforced a shortening of the name to a thriftier, although not necessarily more informative, The Dregs. It was only the first piece of commercially-driven meddling that was to radically alter the direction of the band over the next few years.

Morse accepted the change phlegmatically. He reasoned that 'Dixie' was too redolent of a single musical style, giving a false impression of the band's output: 'A lot of people were saying, "Dixie Dregs, is that a square-dancing or Dixieland band?" We were just trying to let people make up their minds without trying to give them an image.'[54] Yes, there were country and bluegrass influences in their music, but they were less prominent than funk, jazz and, increasingly, rock.

It was thus simply as The Dregs that they put out their next album, *Unsung Heroes*. On one level, the title alludes to its content — music without singing — but it also reflects the way that the band were beginning to see themselves: musicians who were nowhere near as famous as they should have been.

Both meanings are referenced by the cover, which is a monochrome photograph of the band with their mouths airbrushed out. Of the music, Morse is again sole writer as well as producer and he used the handily local Axis Studios in Atlanta. This return-to-roots approach was adopted as part of a switch to an Atlanta-based management company. West suggested that they had been 'ripped off' by their previous managers, so the change was both timely and welcome.[55]

As far as the music is concerned, it is another high energy gallop through various styles, moods, tones... The titles are jokey ('Divided We Stand', anyone?) and everyone gets plenty of solos. 'Cruise Control' is given another pass. Throughout, Morse's playing is typically stellar. On the final track, 'Go For Baroque' (see what they did there?), he makes an acoustic guitar do a passable impression of a harpsichord.

Off the album's back, concert attendances were fine, especially, for some reason, in the New York area. But the hope that the album would earn enough for its creators to be able to work less hard was forlorn. It was well reviewed and achieved the now customary Grammy nomination, but it remained a good distance from the top of the charts.

The next effort, *Industry Standard*, was something of a departure, being far more conventional than much of their work up to that point.

The slightly sarcastic title perhaps indicates their disgruntlement at having to take this route. More personnel shuffling accompanied the recording as Sloan departed in order to begin a career as, of all things, an anaesthesiologist. He was replaced by Mark O'Connor.

For his part, he was happy to be involved, his take on the Dregs being, 'The Dregs were one of the bands I was into, and as soon as I heard them play on stage, I said, "Man, this is the best band I've ever heard." They have everything. Other bands have their individual perfections but this band had it all — country, classical, fusion, the heaviest rock — I just love bass and drums and that was the kick I was looking for.'[56] Morse returned the compliment, saying of O'Connor, 'He was the best violinist I'd ever heard — he played so in tune and so smooth — and that just stuck in my mind.'[57]

Coming immediately after an album that advertised its instrumentals-only content in its title, the inclusion here of vocals on two tracks was the chief novelty. The first 'Crank It Up' features a guest slot from Alex Ligertwood of Santana, who was known to Eddy Offord, the album's producer. It is a fast-paced soft rocker with a riff that is vaguely reminiscent of 'Take It Off The Top.' The second, 'Ridin' High' is funkier and tricksier, with Patrick Simmons from the Doobie Brothers supplying the voice.

Received wisdom is that singing was another demand from Arista, who were still scrambling around for ways to make the band more radio-friendly. That was Morgenstein's take: 'Maybe the vocal thing came about with a meeting with… people on the business side saying, "Guys, what if you maybe get a guest vocalist or two? That might give us a chance that when we shop radio, we could get a few bits and maybe some airplay, which could open up the band to a larger market."'[58]

Morse links it to issues around the change in management: 'It was one of those offers we couldn't turn down. What it was is our manager said he'd let us out of our management contract if we would try the vocals. If it didn't improve our sales, we could get out. That's as hard as you can twist a musician's arm to let them out of a contract! That's a big carrot to hold up, so we of course went for it. But we didn't just say, "Let's put some crappy vocalists on." We got serious and picked people we liked and felt good about the songs.'[59] Whether the track 'Bloodsucking Leeches' has anything to do with all of this is something that only Morse would know.

Another break with tradition was the bringing in of Yes's Steve Howe for a guitar duet on 'Up In The Air,' the punning title of which is presumably partly intended to allude to Morse's love of flying. The track is a beautiful acoustic piece that could provide the backing for a video about some medieval building or other.

Upon release, it was the same old story: good reviews, so-so sales, Grammy nomination. This time, though, it may have contributed to what was arguably Morse's greatest achievement — and the one that would land him his most famous gig a decade later. He was voted Guitarist of the Year for 1982 by the readers of *Guitar Player* magazine. Morse described this as 'the biggest honour he [had] ever had' adding the barbed comment, 'It's an honour to me more than winning a Grammy, because the Grammys are so politically operated.'[60]

Given that *Guitar Player* was aimed squarely at practitioners, it was indeed gratifying that the award was bestowed by readers and not a self-appointed panel. Nothing could better indicate Morse's situation at this stage of his career: lionised by his peers and those who understand what a guitar can and cannot do, but something of a mystery to the public. As Pete Pardo put it, he was a musician's musician who was less feted than the Jimi Hendrixs and Eddie Van Halens of this world, but who could — at least — be ranked with them.[61]

More remarkable than winning the award was the fact that he went on to win it again and again for the following four years, at the end of which the magazine decided that he was no longer eligible. This decision was obviously taken to give someone else a chance, although some excuse was concocted to the effect that, after five straight wins, Morse had achieved a lifetime award.

Whether that first win was meant to or not, it created the suspicion that Morse was now bigger than the band in which he plied his trade. He would not have said so himself: it is impossible to find an opinion about him that dissents from Pardo's judgement that he is, 'Just a normal guy who is obsessed with music and the art of playing guitar.'[62]

Even so, as the chief creative force in the Dregs, it would only have been natural if he had started to feel that there was more he could be doing (although, for the record, he has always stuck to the line that the band gave him plenty of artistic outlets). *Industry*

Standard marked the end of the Dreg's contract with Arista and, tired of the endless touring, they disbanded.

Or rather, they didn't. Morse left — at first to quit the music business, but later to pursue solo ambitions. His take on the split was rooted in the music, 'I've played with the Dixie Dregs for about eleven years, but at a certain point I got the feeling the spirit was no longer there. In all this time, I think we've had vacation for about two weeks, and the band was having a hard time because of drug-related problems of some of the members. On this night, we did a bad gig, which I hate. Next night we played again, followed by another night. That was too much for me, so I stopped.'[63] West has maintained that Arista essentially reneged on a deal to up the production budget every two albums and gave the band a 'like it or lump it' ultimatum. Cut adrift, the Dregs fell apart.

The remaining members drafted in Paul Barrere of Little Feat and gamely kept going for a while, releasing an EP called, imaginatively, *Extended Play*, before calling it a day in 1985. West dialled back his involvement in the music business, going off to work for Pearson, a provider of education services. O'Connor became something of a violin phenomenon, composing with all manner of maestros and travelling the world.

Morgenstein and, briefly, Lavitz would eventually go on to join Morse in a new venture, this time one that made no bones about its chief selling point. Its name? The Steve Morse Band.

5.
Tumeni Notes

In 1983, in the wake of the Dregs' split, Morse added 'journalist' to his list of hyphens. Penning a regular column called 'Open Ears' for the magazine *Guitar for the Practicing Musician* gave him an outlet for all sorts of ideas that purely instrumental music could never accommodate. Unsurprisingly, his contributions were not the exercises in self-apotheosising narcissism that they might have been. He was characteristically modest about his writing: 'My essays have always leaned more toward the philosophy of being a musician rather than just technique. As a writer, I am a novice, but I feel my goal will have been achieved if a positive thought is illuminated when you read what I've got to say. In the long run, I believe that a musician's quality is equal only to his quality as a person.'[64]

As this indicates, the pieces were quite speculative and, where they did deal with a musician's experience, the tone was straightforward and technical, rather than glitzy. A good example would be his two-instalment description of touring in support of Rush, published in 1986, in which, among other things, he wrote:

> 'One of the most asked questions I got on the tour was if I jammed with Alex Lifeson. The answer is no. We spent a lot of time hanging out, but the show was tightly structured. The guy they hired to take care of business and make sure the show didn't go a minute overtime had to have some authority to do his job. It might have cost $5,000 in overtime to jam.'[65]

The focus on the practicalities of putting on a show, the lack of interest in fame, the sly humour — all say much about Morse's priorities. Other topics that he covered as part of his journalistic sideline included the virtues of signing autographs for fans and whether it was valid to argue about who was the greatest guitarist of all time. His conclusion in this case was — again, revealingly — that every guitarist was unique and could not therefore be fairly compared to any other. In many ways, his journalism answers an earlier question: how do we find out about Morse the man when his private life is so, well, private? Easy. Look at what he writes. The evidence is all in there.

As far as playing music was concerned (as opposed to writing about it), the Morse of 1983 was on something of a hiatus. Apart from playing a solo acoustic set as an opener for the trio of Al Di Meola, Paco De Lucia and his hero John McLaughlin at a few of their gigs, he was out of the game. Although according to Russ Devault of the *Atlanta Journal*, it's interesting to note that Morse had auditioned as a possible short-term replacement for Di Meola who had suffered a short illness.

However, Morse turned his attention instead to more banausic occupations. As he said, 'I didn't just quit the band, I quit playing, and I learned how to make a living. I had a farm, and I had a bulldozer. I tried to dig ponds for people and clear trees and bail hay for people... I was just doing anything I could to just not make my living as a musician. I didn't want to quit playing, but I did want to quit the music business.'[66]

It may seem a little odd that someone so devoted to music would give it up for a life that involved none of its creativity (unless digging ponds can be considered creative), but it is wholly consistent with the behaviour that he had displayed throughout his life. It is the same anti-authoritarianism that led him to clash with school superintendents over his hair.

There was some justice to his stance. He had been given plenty of artistic freedom by Capricorn and its eccentric boss, but Arista was an altogether different proposition. Despite his always standing by the albums produced by the shorter named version of his band, the commercial imperative clearly did not sit well with him. But he was not able to go against his essential nature for long; of the simple life he had lapsed into, he said, 'That got old pretty quick.'[67]

In other words, for all the faults of the business that prevented him from jamming with one of his esteemed peers because of potential cost overruns, he began to realise how fortunate he had been to earn his living — such as it was — in music and that, after all, every occupation has its down sides. He could put up with the business elements that he found sordid in order to get more serious about a music career. Some friendly advice from Phil Walden about how to negotiate the commercial side helped to nudge him back towards his true vocation. That said, this would not be the last time that he would leave the industry and turn to a less public means of putting food on the table.

At around the start of his reign as *Guitar Player*'s best of the year, the band that bore his name got together. The reason he did not simply resurrect the Dregs was partly that they were off touring with someone else and partly because of issues around all that pesky business stuff: 'With the Dregs I had a lot of musical control, but the organisation was out of control. No matter what we did or how many records we had out or whatever happened we always just had high overheads and we were on a subsistence type salary, nothing more.'[68]

Having bought the truck that the Dregs had used (which had originally belonged to the Allman Brothers) and worked to get it back into full working order, he remembered a couple of musicians he had seen and thought of getting together a trio. Even if gigs only paid small amounts, it would be enough to buy the fuel needed to keep the show on the road. Over a period of ten years, Morse calculated, it should also pay for his plane.

Initially, the plan — in line with Morse's evident love of a good pun — was to title the new project Morse Code, but that was not available by dint of having been taken by a pre-existing Canadian combo. So, placing his ego front and centre for once, he went with The Steve Morse Band. It made sense. When you are being lauded as the best at what you do, you might as well take that for a spin to see what it can do.

Comprising Morse, Doug Morgan on drums and Jerry Peek on bass, the band made a humble start, appearing at small clubs and gradually building an audience. In the event, Morgan lasted only until the end of a short first tour of the eastern States, never getting to play on any recorded material. Morgenstein was drafted in as a hasty replacement, giving the unmistakable impression that this was a Dregs spin-off project. Morse vehemently resisted this, although he was happy to play Dregs material. Touring took the band to such places as Spartanburg, South Carolina, where they were still booked in to jazz clubs. But they were appreciatively received by audiences and Morse further buffed his public image by giving a free guitar clinic at a place called Parker Music in Wade Hampton Mall.

The band began recording their debut album and embarked on a tour of Germany in early 1984, taking in venues like Batschkapp in Frankfurt, and Ballroom-Blitz in Hannover – a further indication of how Morse was having more impact in Europe than the US. During the tour, he gave more clinics. By July, he was back playing at Beverly Theatre, Los Angeles and its ilk.

That the album, *The Introduction* featured Lavitz on piano reinforced the Dregs connections, as well as taking the band away from its pared-back remit. The guitar legend that was Albert Lee also, like Howe before him, guested on a track. Moreover, Morse augmented his standard role by taking on synthesiser and organ duties. The sonic palette was consequently somewhat larger than would ordinarily be produced by the classic 'power trio' set up.

The label this time was Elektra, or rather their newly launched jazz subsidiary Elektra/Musician. The recordings took place at Morrison Studio in Tampa, Florida, for the lead instruments and Eddy Offord Studio in Atlanta for the drums. As was now usual, everything was written and produced by the band's eponymous front man. It may be that this was the reason for there being no real 'stories' from the recording sessions.

It was not the kind of struggle that has produced many a masterpiece. As Morse said, 'I was producing, but was able to work with great engineers, once again, to make it easy. There was nobody involved with trying to change the music, it was simply "Let's record what we like to do."'[69]

The freedom hinted at here resulted in an album that, for sure, included much that could be expected from a Steve Morse product — the tracks are all instrumentals — but which was much rockier than had been the case with anything in the Dregs' catalogue. The absence of violin and, for the most part, keyboards, meant that arrangements did not need to be quite so firmly nailed down, creating more space for improvisation and the switching around of melodies if the whim took hold.

The Mahavishnu Orchestra was no longer a strong influence, although the Allman Brothers of the 'Jessica' days left trace elements. The opener, 'Cruise Missile,' is based around a Pastorius-like superfast funky riff, but, from there, the album is mainly fuzzbox inflected chords and screeching guitar solos.

The Albert Lee-fortified 'General Lee' (well, why not?) is a succulent slice of Southern fried boogie, 'On The Pipe' and the title track flirt with chugga-chugga heaviness. Lavitz's moment, 'Mountain Waltz' could only come from somewhere below the Mason-Dixon Line. 'The Whistle' is a Bach-like march that originated with Celeste trying and failing to reproduce the theme tune to the film *Bridge on the River Kwai* as she walked to the barn every day, prompting Morse to write her a supposedly easier replacement. Tunes go to unexpected places — a banging rock riff can suddenly give way to a low tempo bit of noodling — but the album has a stylistic unity that is missing from the Dregs' albums.

This could be seen as a natural consequence of losing some instruments, but that would only be half right: it was a deliberate choice, as *The Greenville News* reported in June 1983, 'The Steve Morse Band has a rockier sound because of the simpler configuration of the band [Morse] said, which tends to make it more accessible to the public.'[70] The desire for commercial success was never far from the surface.

Morse appeared optimistic, as he told Russ Devault: 'I've never been one to speculate on that,' he said. 'It depends on a lot of factors beyond my control, and I guess plain old luck is a big part of it. But getting mass exposure is the name of the game, and I sure wouldn't mind if this album got us that exposure. I wouldn't predict it or ever think that, but I've really been surprised to find that Elektra — based on what is happening, which is modest but steady sales — has gone ahead and really pushed the album. I'm shocked by how much airplay it has gotten, and I attribute that to the big push by Elektra.'

The album managed a respectable, but hardly blockbusting, 101 on the billboard 200 chart, although it did get to 15 on the Jazz chart, despite being arguably the least jazzy recording that Morse had put out so far. Not helping was the fact that Elektra/Musician abruptly folded in 1984 when its head, Bruce Lundvall, went to EMI to start their Manhattan label. For the band, another tour of Germany beckoned, but their problems around releasing their material were far from over.

'The way I see it,' he said, 'we have to be able to sell the music live before we can sell records. Sometimes when you're tired and haven't slept and are just plain tired of travelling, you wish it wasn't that way, but you've got to sell people before they'll buy the record.'

'Part of my lifestyle involves not depending on the albums for success. I know that sounds defeatist, but it's not. To me that's the most optimistic view. That way you can do what you like (in the recording studio) and what you believe in, and that's what music is all about.'

The next album, *Stand Up*, recalled *Industry Standard* by incorporating vocals. This time, singing was even more pervasive, four of the nine tracks including lyrics. Again, the core trio was augmented by guests. Familiar faces Lavitz and O'Connor popped in to provide cameos. Lee was back, this time both singing and playing on the aptly named 'Rocking Guitars,' and Ligertwood sang on the title track.

As an artistic product, it takes forward the sound of *The Introduction*, although the vocals give more of an impression of novelty than is actually the case. Musically, it could not be mistaken for the work of anyone but Morse. It is rocky, but it also sounds very of its time. It was released in 1985, but anyone who did not know that could easily guess. The complex bass lines, stabbing synths and earnest, anthemic vocals that were de rigueur for a certain type of soft rock at the time, are all present and correct.

Whether it was this album or an accumulation of music over a period of years that attracted Rush and their 'people' is difficult to say, but the offer of a supporting slot on the Power Windows Tour was a huge deal — although it would prove to be significant in Morse's career for entirely the wrong reasons.

For a start, it meant the humility of being low on the bill, although, as Morse acknowledged, the opportunity for wide exposure was priceless. Morse and colleagues were granted a thirty-five-minute slot, which absolutely had to end on time — regardless of whether it started late. Long solos, then, were out, as were acoustic songs, or anything else that would require stopping the show to set up. The venues were larger than the band had hitherto been accustomed to and the acoustics did not always favour instrumental music. Given all of this, it was decided to aim for high energy and play some of the rockier songs from the repertoire. 'Cruise Missile' and 'Cruise Control' were in, as was 'Stand Up,' which allowed for an audience singalong, facilitated by the tour singer Terry Brock.

Morse's first meeting with the members of Rush only happened the night before the opening gig. The two bands were rehearsing and took the opportunity to introduce themselves to each other. It was the beginning of an enjoyable personal association. Morse said that Rush were generous with their time, answering questions, providing help and socialising. Morse even got to combine several enthusiasms by flying Alex Lifeson from one gig to another.

4th December 1985 was when the first performance of The Steve Morse Band as a support act took place, the setting being Portland, Maine. It went well, the band garnering some favourable reviews. The *Kennebec Journal*, for example, had this to say about their 'all too short seven song set':

> 'It was encouraging to see a healthy amount of "Steve Morse Band" t-shirts out in the crowd as well as hearing people scream his name that night for he's another one of the premiere guitarists in the rock world today!'[71]

But it would be a mistake to see this as a moment of triumph for Morse. It was far from that. The tour should have been the pinnacle of his career to date, but it rapidly turned into a disaster. As he slogged around in the wake of his megastar benefactors, Morse learned that Elektra, anticipating low sales, were declining to release *Stand Up* on the new-fangled CD format that was then sweeping the world — which, naturally, guaranteed that their prophecy would be self-fulfilling. Worse, they ended their support — mainly of the financial variety — for the tour, which meant that Morse, as band leader, was liable for any further costs. As he said, 'I was faced with a huge loss keeping my word to everybody, and making their salaries, and finishing the tour or just cancelling. So, I finished the tour and was deeply in debt for that and really, really, really, really bitter.'[72]

The optimism and promise that had attended the formation of The Steve Morse Band was ebbing away. Cut adrift by his record company, Morse was also facing personnel problems; Morgenstein had moved to New York, which made him less readily available. Plus, he was being wooed by other artists eager to secure his services. It was becoming obvious that his commitment to future projects could not be guaranteed — if such projects ever even got off the ground.

A fresh approach was needed, although perhaps not something quite so drastic as quitting to become a farmer. An indication of Morse's thinking was the retirement of the Frankenstein Telecaster, or, rather, its augmentation and replication. It had been with him for his entire career to date and had been a central element in his signature sound, but nothing can be expected to keep going forever.

Partnering with Ernie Ball Music Man, Morse helped to produce a custom guitar that was effectively an authorised copy of the Frankenstein, albeit a copy that was properly manufactured and not cobbled together using chisels from the garage of Morse's father and the scavenged components of several other instruments.

The Steve Morse custom guitar boasted four pick-ups that gave any number of sound options without recourse to effects boxes or pedals. Flick the switch and it could blast out raw noise, flick it again and the clean notes of a more classical style bounced gaily in the air. An important feature was a tone control that changed the sound, rather than simply adding to it or taking away from it. Morse took full advantage of that; in future years, he would habitually play a chord and then roll the tone control to remove some of the top as the singer joined in. That was for the future. For now, a new guitar was not the only change that Morse made. He also had some new picks made to celebrate his wedding on 1st June 1986. On one side they simply read, 'Steve and Celeste Morse 6-1-86' and on the other side: 'official wedding pick.'

These weren't the only significant events at the time. Steve also did what he had not done since the far-off days of The Plague: he joined someone else's band.

6.
Arena Rock

Kansas' 1986 album *Power* came after something of a hiatus for the band and featured a largely new line-up, of one of whom co-founder Rich Williams has said, 'I was sitting down with Steve and he had just been awarded the best guitar player ever for the third year in a row and here I am in a room with him and we're creating material together. For me, that was a terrifying experience, until I got to know what Steve was like. He's the least threatening and intimidating guy you could ever meet. He's a guitar wizard.'[73]

The Steve in question was, of course, Morse. In Williams, we hear again the voice of a peer who admired Morse, even as the general public continued to give him a shoulder that was, if not exactly cold, lukewarm at best. Before meeting Williams, Morse had been kicking around, doing the thing that he did. He had supported Joe Zawinul on his Dialects tour, playing classical guitar and other pieces over a looped backing. That connection was made by Jaco Pastorius, who had worked with Zawinul in the jazz fusion Weather Report. Among the stops was Carnegie Hall, where Peter Frampton joined Morse for a song. The whole thing was, Morse averred, an 'intense' experience during which he did not form much of a relationship with Zawinul, who tended to keep himself separate.

As far as Kansas was concerned, Morse's involvement happened almost by accident. Having scored a complimentary seat for a Robert Plant gig, he found himself seated next to Phil Ehart, Kansas' drummer, who, among other things, mentioned that the band was thinking of getting together, but minus Kerry Livgren, the guitarist. Livgren's conversion to evangelical Christianity had become a problem, as it had started to influence the band's lyrics — much to the disgust of some of the other members, who, perhaps understandably, did not want to be in a religious band. As Morse reported it, 'So I said [to Ehart] "Hey if you need any help — I'd love to write tunes with you guys or something", and he said "Yeah — we were actually thinking about that!" so it was "Great — let's do it!" So, we just ended up writing an album together.'[74]

True to form, Morse was a major creative influence on what ended up coming of this. He teamed up with lead vocalist and keyboard player Steve Walsh — who was himself returning to the band after a period away forced by 'artistic differences' — to write almost all of the tracks. A few credits go to others, mostly non-members of the band, but the core duo was in more-or-less total control of the process. Walsh was glowing about his new collaborator: 'Melody is my favourite thing, but I don't have a real gift for melody. Steve Morse does. He's a truly gifted guitarist. I first met him in Atlanta when we moved down here about eight years ago. I heard his band (the Dixie Dregs) and they were awesome. We've kind of known each other since then.'[75]

Ehart and Andrew Powell were on production duties this time, leaving Morse to focus on writing and playing. It was an interesting combination, the Englishman Powell having a very academic background and experience in writing and performing classical music. In the pop world, he had briefly been a member of the Alan Parsons Project and had produced Kate Bush's early efforts. The recording studios that were used were equally broad in scope: the band recorded in Tennessee, whereas orchestral backing (presumably Powell's contribution) was laid down at Abbey Road in London. The label was MCA — which — natch — would quickly become a bugbear for Morse.

Power represented a change for Morse in being heavily reliant on vocals. One track, the distinctly Steve Morse Band-sounding, 'Musicatto,' is instrumental, but everything else is a song with lyrics and a repetitive structure and — basically, all of the things that Morse had been avoiding for most of his career. Of course, he had written songs with vocals before, but they had been exceptions to the general music-only rule.

This new album was by far his most full-blooded excursion into sung territory so far. It was also unequivocally rock, albeit in a poppy vein. Listening to it now is to be transported back to a time when music and technology had yet to come to any kind of amicable agreement about which was going to do what. So, Morse grinds away on his guitar, supplying some heavy lines and riffs that are only slightly leavened by the very dated sounding synths and electric pianos that are a big part of the arrangements. Yes are an obvious influence, as are frankly just about any other MOR band of the 80s. Pompous chuggers alternate with over-earnest power ballads of the type that Heart and Journey could just about pull off but which do not wholly convince here.

None of this is to say that it is absolutely terrible. It is very well played and Walsh was right about melody — it is undoubtedly melodic. From the high-octane opener, 'Silhouettes In Disguise,' to the 'Eye Of The Tiger'-ish title track, to the mid-paced, 'Tomb 19,' it bowls along pleasantly enough. But none of it sounds particularly original or fresh. It is an album with little identity of its own. Only 'Musicatto' and the acoustic 'Taking In The View' remind the listener of the full range of Morse's compositional dexterity.

Reviews were not, for the most part, too kind. The British heavy rock magazine *Kerrang!* called most of the album 'embarrassing,' while more recent commentators, looking at it retrospectively, all pick up on one major point: it does not sound like Kansas.

Once again, Morse blamed the record company, 'When I got with them,' he said in 1990, 'I envisaged that they would sound more like the old Kansas (of the 1970s) because I have very strong instrumental leanings. But I'd say more record company pressure made it lean more toward the pop song category. It's no one's fault.'[76]

This was something that happened a lot in the mid-80s: it was, after all, the age in which commercially-minded media conglomerates decided that classic artists, such as Tina Turner, Jethro Tull and Fleetwood Mac, should all sound the same — that is, like something that would appeal to those arbiters of what could succeed and what could not, MTV and its consumers.

Power was somewhat unusual for Morse in being not well received by the critics but lapped up by the public. A solid hit as an album, climbing to 35 on the US Billboard 200 chart, it spawned a hit single, the 'synth-based and relatively mellow,'[77] 'All I Wanted,' which reached a lofty 19 on the Billboard Hot 100 chart — the last time that Kansas appeared anywhere close to that high up. For Morse as an individual, these successes presumably did something to ease the financial pain from the Rush debacle.

They also 'power'ed, a lengthy period on the road that carried the band through into 1987. The first concerts were as part of a USO 1st Airborne Rock and Roll division tour that took in military bases around the world, including some of those in East Asia, Europe and Iceland. Morse has spoken about how this called for the band to travel by helicopter from one aircraft carrier to another entertaining the sailors. It is to be wondered how Morse's hair went down in such places.

Set lists from this time show that the new songs received some exposure,[78] but much of the average gig's runtime was taken up with older material. Typical was that from the Riverside Theatre Milwaukee on 17th April, which included a good sprinkling of *Power* tracks but reverted to the old stagers when it became necessary to appease an impatient audience. To be fair, Morse was able to sneak in 'Up In The Air,' but there was no dislodging the ever present, 'Dust In The Wind,' Kansas' best-known song, which pre-dated his membership. It was all a premonition of a situation that still lay some years in the future, during which the indispensable song would have a strangely similar title...

Williams learned something of Morse's unique mindset while on tour. Returning to their hotel after a show, they came across an undistinguished local band in the lounge. 'I was about to make a joke about it,' Williams has said, 'when Steve turned to me and said, "Did you see what the guitar player just did there?" It was something that the player did with his toggle switch. Steve said he had never seen anybody do it that way before. I thought, "He is the best guitar player in the world, and he is still always learning." He was looking for something that was different like this kid did in that band.'[79]

In the wake of *Power* Morse made the sudden, and rather strange, decision to once again leave behind music, this time to follow his other great love: he became a full-time commercial airline pilot, working for Atlantic Southeast Airlines. Perhaps this should not come as too much of a shock, but it was at least idiosyncratic coming so soon after he had finally made some commercial headway in music.

It possibly says a lot about his state of mind at the time, with the Rush tour still relatively recent and his having gone against type by joining a pre-existing band. To darken the mood further, he lost another of his old gang when Jaco Pastorius died as a result of being beaten by a bouncer at a nightclub in Florida.

The airline was regional, mainly operated in the South and, for part of its history, focussed on the commuter trade. Most of its fleet consisted of Embraer EMB 110 Bandeirantes, which were small, propellor 'planes designed for short hops. As a job, it was a chance for Morse to utilise a major skill set. He had, after all, long been carrying rock 'n' rollers, so why not businessmen? His plan was to advance sufficiently in his career as to maximise his earning power, giving him a financial safety net that would make the playing of gigs every now and then less of a gamble.

Morse's take on his new direction was, 'Being a pilot was neat because you have regularity about your work and you have a chance of doing your job in a very finite and finished way. When you're done, you're done. It's not like you have to agonise over everything — you've done your job and you can put it out of your mind until the next day. With music, the days don't seem to have any separation. One of the biggest differences is time — you spend the day flying and get off work and you're done.'[80]

The rumour that he had Velcro attached to his trousers and the steering wheel of his car so that he could navigate with his legs on his journey to work — the better to practise guitar while driving — remains just that, a rumour, albeit an enjoyable one.

In the event, the job did not last for long. 'I won't be going back to working as a commercial pilot,' he has confirmed, 'I pretty much burned that bridge when I retired -after six months. Resigning from a job is not a particularly good thing to put on your resume. But I found that as much as I enjoyed the flying, the rest of it — wearing a uniform, keeping up the paperwork — was just a job. I missed the unpredictability of a music career.'[81]

As with his earlier foray into farming, he was ultimately unable to deny his true vocation: music. It was far from the end of his love affair with flying. He even claimed that it benefited his music, giving him that bigger view that put heart into what he created. Flying, he has said, has a level of artistic performance to it; a pilot's quest for perfection is identical to that of a practising musician. For all that, it is interesting that he mentions clothing in his list of reasons for feeling constrained. It seemed that, somewhere inside him, could still be found the boy protesting the rules around hair at his school. It was not to be the last time that dress codes would be a potential dealbreaker.

His other job — with the band — moved to the forefront again, when it came time to make a follow-up to *Power*. *In The Spirit Of Things* took Kansas even further down the road of novelty — not always to good effect. The most obvious positive development was that it brought into Morse's life a figure who would become more and more influential some three decades later, the producer Bob Ezrin.

Already a legend thanks largely to producing the likes of Kiss, Aerosmith and Alice Cooper, not to mention the cultural landmark that was Pink Floyd's *The Wall*, Ezrin was a cerebral and highly exacting presence who had as much impact on the artistry of an album as the musicians it was nominally all about. He was not one to settle for sloppy production values or lazily written songs.

As bassist Billy Greer has said, 'He really held our feet to the fire in making sure the lyrics were up to snuff. And Steve [Walsh] being the main lyric writer at the time, he was the one that felt the most pressure.'[82] Indeed, Walsh, while praising Ezrin, described the process of working with him as quite gruelling. Greer maintained that Ezrin was 'really fun to work with'[83] and Williams said that 'working with Bob Ezrin was an honour. Bob was in total control but was never a jerk about it. Bob is an ideas guy and with all his experience, he never was lacking in ideas or opinions.'[84]

As for Morse? His view was not dissimilar: '[Ezrin] is like the designated chairman of the board when it comes to discussions. He throws in his opinion, but it carries a little bit more weight because he's done so many great albums. He's also one of the smartest guys you'll ever meet in terms of memorising the complicated details of a tune and what you played within it.'[85]

Much of what made Ezrin so special was his creative approach to production; for him, mics and tape were not merely ways to record sounds, but resources to be exploited — almost instruments in their own right. For example, he set up the drums in the studio with a PA system in such a way that the natural compression of the room contributed to the overall effect. He also punched in to recordings, going back to places where a mistake had been made to put it right, an easy enough thing to do in these days of digital, but revolutionary when the medium was two-inch tape.

Not just a producer, Ezrin was an excellent musician and he contributed to the writing of several songs. To some extent, the effect was to crowd out Morse. For sure, the two Steves were still the album's core songwriting team, but other names appear in the credits — several songs have no input from Morse or Walsh at all.

Another break with tradition is the fact that the album has a loose unifying concept, since it impressionistically tells the story of how the town of Neosho Falls in the state of — does it need to be said? — Kansas was devastated by a flood in 1951. This idea came to Williams after he read a book about lost towns in the state. Walsh and Ehart visited in 1988 and were amazed to find a place that people had left — and never returned to. Shops were still stocked, houses were still furnished; it had everything a town should have, except for people.

People had, in fact, been at the heart of the original plan for the album, which had been to centre each song on a specific individual. It was Ezrin who suggested placing them all in the same place, Neosho Falls fitting well. The narrative frame is most obvious in the opening song, 'Ghosts,' the lyrics of which are filled with images of destruction and abandonment. Walsh claimed that he wrote it during that visit to the town: 'Just from looking around and noticing [the town] and envisioning and imagining.'[86]

Upon the album's release in October 1988, reviews were — and continue to be — sniffy. *The Daily Illini* praised it as 'very well executed with a great deal of style,' but lamented that the overall effect was ruined by 'three weak tracks, all in sequence, smack dab in the middle of the album.'[87] The *Gazette* was considerably less generous, bemoaning Morse's lack of presence and labelling Walsh's vocals 'stunningly banal.'[88] Ouch! All Music's Stephen Erlewine, writing retrospectively, called the album 'doggedly sombre' and opined that, 'the cavernous, DDD-wannabe production screams 1988.'[89]

To compound its critical reception, the album was a commercial stinker. Managing a lowly 114 on the Billboard 200 chart, it did not stick around for long. The single 'Stand Beside Me' got to 13 on the Mainstream Rock charts but left consolidated charts entirely untroubled. Ironically, the unifying concept had been deliberately introduced as a way to interest record buyers who might have felt jaded by the endless parade of love songs that filled release schedules. It resolutely did not work.

Much of the blame can be laid, not for the first time, on a

lack of record company support. It is true that a glossy video was produced for the single, which found its way on to MTV, but other promotional efforts were half-hearted at best. MCA had simply lost interest, having made a decision to drop 'older' acts in favour of younger artists who were deemed more commercial (there is no point in naming any of these since most are now forgotten — unlike Kansas). Despite being barely in his thirties, Morse was firmly in the 'oldie' camp.

That having been said, the album itself cannot be entirely let off the hook. It is even more starkly of its time than *Power*. On occasion (e.g.: 'One Big Sky'), the band could be mistaken for a John Farnham tribute act. The rest of it is yet more lightly distorted guitars, synths, complicated bass lines, big choruses and anguished ballads. It is not unentertaining in parts and it would be a physical impossibility to put those musicians and that producer into a room together without producing something very, very competent. And, yes, as backing music for a break-up montage featuring Molly Ringwald and Andrew McCarthy, it would be perfect. But, in any other context, it sounds so dated that it is hard to imagine it ever sounding of the moment.

Walsh argued that the album's success, or lack thereof, did not bother him because it was the artistic statement that he wanted it to be. For him, it was about reconnecting with his Midwest roots: he felt that in recent years, the band has lost its way and forgotten who they were. Maybe that was the case, but the harsh reality was that *In The Spirit Of Things* was their last release for years, their last on a major label and their last to feature Steve Morse.

7.
The Road Home

Morse had a history of providing guitar parts for musicians as a guest player. A notable example was a special appearance on a Lynyrd Skynyrd tribute album, made in 1987. Timed to commemorate the tenth anniversary of the 'plane crash that had claimed the lives of several members of the original band, it included those who remained, the brother of the vocalist Ronnie Van Zant (who had been among the dead) and a long list of invited musicians. It was released the following year as *Southern By The Grace Of God: Lynyrd Skynyrd Tribute Tour 1987*.

Morse credits this session with rescuing him from the routine of life as an airline pilot. It started when, at two o'clock in the morning after a gruelling day in the cockpit, he received an unexpected call: 'On the phone was [Lynyrd Skynyrd guitarist] Gary Rossington, who said, "Hey, we're down at the [Atlanta indoor arena] Omni. Man, you gotta come down. Bring your guitar. We're recording tonight."'[90]

Morse's initial response was, 'I've been at work all day and I cut off all my hair.'[91] Asked to turn up at six (presumably AM), he did not make it, but 'I [finally] got there. They're already playing. They look over and Gary gets the message that I'm here. He says, "All right, everybody, we're gonna bring up Steve Morse to play on the song, "Gimme Back My Bullets."'[92] Morse did his bit and, while doing so, began to feel that being in the music industry was cool after all.

Even more momentously, the Dixie Dregs (under their shortened name of Dregs) were resurrected in 1988 for a tour and to record a demo for a make of synthesiser. The three-track CD single was given the appropriate title of *Off The Record* and featured new recordings of 'Leprechaun Promenade' and 'Take It Off The Top' plus a nine-minute band interview.

The line-up featured Morse, Morgenstein, Lavitz and Sloan,

differences presumably settled, or schedules cleared. West did not return, his place being taken by Dave LaRue, who was brought in on Lavitz's recommendation. In fact, LaRue was involved with a number of bands and would routinely play with one band one night and another the next.

The full range of the Dregs' albums was represented on stage, but there was no new material: it was to be a long time before the band would get back into the studio. The reunion was an enjoyable enough experience for all involved, but the extent to which it influenced a decision that Morse was soon to take is hard to say.

As for Kansas, low sales notwithstanding, *In The Spirit Of Things* needed to be publicised somehow and that meant live performances. Starting on 2nd January in Puerto Rico, Morse and Co spent a good proportion of the first half of 1989 on the road. The new album was not as well represented in the setlist as might have been expected, only a handful of tracks sharing runtime with the classics. The show on 14th February was recorded for the syndicated radio show *King Biscuit Flower Hour*. It was released in 1998 as a live album, with two tracks from the original broadcast missing (one being an easily dispensed with cover of 'Born To Be Wild').

The tour ended in April in Germany, at which point an exasperated Morse quit. Of his time in Kansas, he commented, 'It was an exercise in teamwork, which I wasn't that good at, coming from always having total control. So, I learned a lot. The tours were really great, but the whole big picture got lost. Personally, I felt the idea we had for the band wasn't executed the best way possible. Also, I missed what I had been doing all my life — making my own music. So, I wanted to get back to it.'[93] This is more than slightly disingenuous given how much of the two Kansas albums had comprised Morse compositions, but clearly something had to give and that something was Morse.

Not one to rest on his laurels, or mope over disappointments, he quickly released a solo album, *High Tension Wires* (as it happens, for MCA). Although it was put out under his name alone (the 'Band' bit was dropped), it was something of a homecoming that brought back many of his old collaborators: Morgenstein, West, Lavitz, Peek and Sloan all appeared.

A lush set of acoustic-driven tracks, titles such as 'Country Colors,' 'Highland Wedding' and (a remade) 'Leprechaun Promenade' give a sense of the genres covered. Often cited as Morse's best album,

High Tension Wires made no real dent in the charts, as much as it says a lot about his apparent desire to move on — or back; to make a change, anyway. Not only did he release the album, but he cut his hair short!

The next album, *Southern Steel* from 1991, saw the restoration of the Steve Morse Band name, Morse now being supplemented by Van Romaine on drums and Dave LaRue on bass. It was exactly the return to creative control that he claimed had been missing from the Kansas experience — not that he ruled out getting the most out of his gifted collaborators: 'I made it clear to the members that I write all the songs, but I said "I want you to tell me what you like and what you don't like and I'll give you stuff to work on and come up with your own versions of the parts I give you." It was a departure for me to have the band actively change the music.'[94]

The result was an album that could be filed without hesitation under 'heavy rock.' It is, obviously, vocal-free and the title is fair in hinting at a Southern twang to many of the tracks, but riffs and solos dominate. That is not to say that there is an absence of subtleties — it is Morse, after all, and plenty of styles are referenced. But it is generally a contrast to the folky, Celtic twiddling of *High Tension Wires* and could hardly be less like the slick-but-empty corporate rock of the two Kansas albums. Nothing could more clearly point to the turn that Morse's career would take a few short years later, in both its sound and the manner of its composition.

In the wake of the album's release, Morse's family expanded as he fathered a son. The happy event provoked some introspection on his part of a type that would become a theme in his utterances: 'It's changed my view about touring for sure and I have a difficult time reconciling that I always want to tour with the fact that I miss my little boy the minute I leave. So, I have to figure a way to tour where I can take a smaller chunk of time and more frequent breaks.'[95]

It was perhaps understandable that Morse felt this way. He was by now nearly twenty years into a musical career and much, it must be said, was going right. He received the general approbation of critics and commentators and the Grammy Award nominations spoke for themselves. The ultimate accolade of his five-year run as the world's best guitarist was unbeatable. From an artistic perspective, he had finally found a group of musicians with whom he would enjoy a long term collaboration: the line-up that produced

Southern Steel appeared on its successor, *Coast To Coast* and became regulars on stage. Sales of his work were okay — sometimes. Yet, for all that, he remained relatively obscure to the public at large. *Coast To Coast* made number 30 on the Billboard Heatseekers Chart, which had been specifically established to showcase new and developing artists: it was a weird listing for someone who by now had some fifteen albums to his credit.

If he was beginning to reach the conclusion that his career was only one part of his life, who can blame him? He was generally satisfied with what he was doing to the level that he was doing it; as he said: '*High Tension Wires* was one of the experiments I always wanted to do and I felt happy with the results and the stuff with the band has been great. The *Coast To Coast* album I think really captures what we're about and the same with the stuff on *Southern Steel*.'[96]

The title of *Coast To Coast* was inspired by Morse's move from California — where he had recently been living — to his old stamping ground of Florida. He had been in California because he was trying to be a 'real writer' turning out music for films: 'It turns out I went too far away. I went to a remote place and I was flying my little plane to LA, to Santa Monica. I thought that was good enough, but [the film company] wanted somebody right there, somebody who could be there and come down and edit this part and if you were going on gigs they just didn't want to work. They wanted the writer/arranger to always be on call. So, all right, that whole thing didn't work out — for a lot of reasons.'[97]

He had been having a house built in Ocala, Florida, for, as he put it, less in total than the legal and admin fees alone would have cost him in California. A main purpose for moving was to go into the hay farming business, but a studio was included in the design.

Annoyingly, it was not completed when Morse was first thinking about *Coast To Coast*, so he started recording the album in a makeshift studio in California before renting a truck, packing all of his equipment into it and driving the 3500 miles to Florida.

When he arrived, the studio was still not ready, so he set up an ad hoc facility in his garage; as he explained: 'I did the guitar parts after I moved. So, we started in California while my studio was getting built here in Florida. I finished the album in my new garage. It was just crazy. The guitar parts were done in a little U-Haul trailer just outside the garage — that was funny.'[98] The album's title was thus as much about the process of its own making as any theme or central idea.

As for its contents, it is another eclectic collection, with a by now customary leaning towards the heavy. Some of the songs sound instrumental as though by the default of an engineer having forgotten to mix in the singer. The opener, 'User Friendly,' for example, has a strong, catchy riff and 'verse' sections that could easily support a vocal line. Lyricism and loveliness are the order of the day on 'Get It In Writing.' 'Morning Rush Hour' is another one that sounds not unlike 'Take It Off The Top' in places.

AllMusic's retrospective review is positive, stating that, 'All of the ten songs on this record are short, with only one clocking in at over four minutes, but Morse has packed a lot into each of them. They are multi-layered, with many different themes and melodies, each building to a logical conclusion.'[99] The kicker, though, is that regardless of its excellence, the review states that the album is not as essential as Morse's work with the Dixie Dregs.

Such a comment references the constant stream of questions that Morse was forced to field about whether the Dregs would get back together again and, more specifically, release any new material. While publicising *Southern Steel* he addressed the issue: 'Another reunion maybe, but we have to keep it short because we all have other things to do. I don't want to do a quick, crappy record just to make a little money. I've learned that if anything is easy now, you'll pay for it later.'[100]

When it did happen, the reason was somewhat surprising. The 1988 experiment had been catalysed by a compilation called *The Best Of The Dregs: Divided We Stand.*

Now, the spur was the unlikely rebirth of Capricorn Records under the irrepressible Phil Walden. Having spent his time since the previous collapse maintaining a low-key career as a talent manager, he signed a partnership deal with Warner Brothers in 1991 to bring the label back and proceeded to operate out of the music capital that is Nashville. In what seems like a case of nominative determinism, the first act signed was the Georgia band Widespread Panic (the membership of which included one T. Lavitz).

With the Dixie Dregs, things got going with a live album, *Bring 'Em Back Alive.* Morse described how this came about: 'It obviously has the advantage or disadvantage of having a lot of pressure during the time you record, which was two nights early in the tour in Atlanta. It also had the advantage of taking less time to get a finished product — the only way we could have done an album at that time. We were fortunate that Capricorn was into it.'[101]

An anecdote from the production of this album gives a small insight into Morse the family man. On one occasion, his toddler son was with him and, as toddlers are wont to do, he was fiddling around with the buttons on the mixer desk. Pressing the wrong one, he caused a few seconds of drums to be erased from the recording. Not one to lose his cool, Morse gave his son something to do to while he searched for a patch — a few seconds of drums that could be spliced in to cover the gap. He found one — it took some hours, but he managed it — and used the primitive digital technology of the time to make good the mistake. Somewhere on the album is a moment that is not strictly speaking authentic, but no one is likely to notice it.

The next release was a studio album, *Full Circle*, the Dregs' first since *Industry Standard* over a decade earlier. The classic line-up featured — sort of. LaRue continued on bass, but there was no Sloan this time. In an almost-as-good outcome, violin duties were covered by Jerry Goodman, erstwhile stalwart of the Mahavishnu Orchestra.

It was a happy arrangement despite, as Goodman pointed out, his approach not always being what Morse was expecting: 'I think I was a little over the top for him in my sonic choices. "Do you always play with distortion in Mahavishnu?" "No, but I'm doing it now!"'[102]

As Morse has pointed out, Goodman's sound was closer to heavy metal than the more traditional violin playing of Sloan. It added new dimensions, although Goodman has noted that almost every band that Morse has put together has mirrored the instrumentation of the Mahavishnu Orchestra: a violin has been ever-present, regardless of its suitability to the style being played.

Full Circle amply demonstrates this. It has all the variety of a typical Dregs work, but the abiding feeling is heavy. A far cry from the early days, it would be a strange entry on a jazz chart. Songs such as 'Aftershock' and 'Perpetual Reality' are straightforward examples of riff-laden rock.

As was now customary, Morse produced and wrote almost all the music, the one exception being an instrumental cover of The

Yardbirds' 'Shapes Of Things,' which is an enjoyable take on what was turning into a rock standard. It came about, as Morse said when, 'We were just throwing out ideas. I had to actually write some new parts for it to add enough energy to make it a Dregs tune. I didn't know if that would be considered heresy or not. We just did it anyway.'[103]

Whether or not the album reflected any residual Kansas influence is, in many ways, irrelevant, but a sense that the Dregs were ploughing a furrow that was increasingly returning a low yield was unavoidable. In an astute review, Ben Edmonds of the *Detroit Free Press* asked: 'Now that fusion is no longer an issue, where do the Dixie Dregs fit into 1994? Some may say that this is arena rock light, but I can see a whole new world for Morse and Pals to explore: call it New Age with an attitude.'[104]

It was a good question. Josef Woodard in the *Los Angeles Times* proposed an answer: 'The Dregs fit nowhere except in their own niche. There's no inherent jazz connection or rhythmic feel that would align them to the fusion field. Radio airplay eludes them, except when their music is used as pads under commercials.'[105]

Morse was by now inclined to accept this: 'There's no question about the fact that we're underground. Obviously, we're not as angst-ridden as some of the current bands that are underground.'[106]

The Full Circle tour took up most of the year and saw the band travel all over the USA. It was generally a success, even if it did nothing to move the dial on Morse's lack of radio-friendliness. Reviews were, as ever, positive; *The Buffalo News* reported: 'The Dixie Dregs started Friday's show with "Aftershock" from the newly released CD, *Full Circle*. Loud cheers from the musician crowd followed each song. An always smiling Morse easily displayed his diversity in styles — from the country picking tune "Blood Sucking Leeches" to the melodic version of the Yardbirds' classic "Shapes Of Things."'[107] Similar accolades were accorded the band wherever they appeared.

So, it was 1994 and Steve Morse was playing again with the Dixie Dregs, living again in Florida and writing, still, for the *Practicing Musician* magazine. He had moved away from being merely influenced by the Mahavishnu Orchestra to having appropriated one of its members for his own band. Full circle indeed.

He was as active as ever in lending his talents to other artists: he played on Michael Manring's *Thonk*, on two tracks, 'Snakes Got Legs' and 'You Offered Only Parabolas'. It was an experience of which he said, 'It was a surprise to be invited to do that because Michael was from another part of the business that was more celebrated and welcomed by the media. I was surprised that he wanted a weird guy like me to put his music into a different place.'[108]

And perhaps that equilibrium could have been maintained, with Morse's career carrying on in the same old way for the foreseeable — and maybe the unforeseeable — future. But a glass of water thrown thousands of miles away by someone he had never met, at someone else he had never met, was about to change everything forever.

8.
The Purpendicular Waltz

In 1993, Deep Purple were at their lowest ebb, nine years into a reunion that had been tumultuous to say the least. Disharmony between lead guitarist Ritchie Blackmore and vocalist Ian Gillan had been an undercurrent since the earliest days, but it had recently flared up to the point at which they were barely prepared to acknowledge each other's existence.

The band's twenty fifth anniversary had been marked by the release of a disappointing album appropriately titled, *The Battle Rages On...* and while it was being toured, a concert at the NEC in Birmingham UK was marred by Blackmore seeming to throw a glass of water at Gillan. The guitarist later claimed that the actual target had been a video cameraman who had been standing too close and putting him off his music.

Roadie Colin Hart had a different take: 'That whole incident was really stupid and Blackmore knew there would be a cameraman over on [keyboard player] Jon [Lord's] side of the stage. I had been to his house to discuss camera positions etc. even before the tour started. The water mostly hit Ian Gillan's wife Bron and afterwards, I thought there would be more trouble, but Ian was the gentleman through it all.'[109]

Be that as it may, there was no going back and Blackmore left, finishing off a few European dates before rather presumptuously declaring an East Asia leg cancelled. His colleagues refused to go along with that and drafted in Joe Satriani to take his place. To everyone's surprise (and, no doubt, relief) this proved an exceptionally felicitous move, audiences responding rapturously to the renewed energy on display. So successful was the arrangement that Satriani, who had initially committed only to completing the 1993 tour, stuck around for further gigs the following year. Unfortunately, that was it for him. When offered a permanent berth, he respectfully declined, making the good (and, as it turned out, prescient) argument that no-one would be able to replace Blackmore and that it would be folly to even try.

What, then, to do? The legend is that the remaining four members of the band each made a wish list of possible replacements, and one name appeared at the top of every one: Steve Morse. Mmm… It is a nice story and, as the often-misquoted line goes, when presented with the truth or the legend, print the legend. If nothing else, it reinforces any claim of unanimity. This was, after all, a perilous time. Replacing Blackmore was not just the bringing in of a stand-in or short-term replacement; for many fans, Blackmore was Deep Purple.

If there were to be a future, whoever the band got needed to be white-hot musically, high in standing and presented as the only choice with no dissenting voices. With this in mind, Morse became Deep Purple's number one target.

Irrespective of motive, the choice was far from a natural one. Deep Purple were a classic hard rock band — among the greatest ever exponents of their genre — and had rarely shown much appetite to compromise on that. Their music was a world away from what Morse had been producing for pretty much all of his career. For sure, some of the riffs on later Steve Morse Band albums sounded a bit like they could have been written by Deep Purple, but his fusion leanings were definitely not what was required. On top of that, Purple were decidedly vocal driven. Gillan, with tongue superglued to inside of cheek, would go on to state that they were an instrumental band with vocal accompaniment, but the few out-and-out instrumentals that they had produced were mainly from line-ups that did not feature him — excepting improvised jams produced for radio sessions.

They were also British. They had enjoyed considerable success in the US in the early 70s and at the start of the reunion in 1985, but their star had long since faded over there. Any new member would have to accept that most of their touring would take place elsewhere.

From Morse's side, the main issue was around creative control. Having manoeuvred himself into the position of having exactly what he wanted, he was on the verge of throwing it all away to become just another band member again. The last time that he had tried that, with Kansas, the results had been less than satisfactory.

But, even then, he had at least been the main composer. Purple's approach was more democratic: their songs were not 'composed' as such. Instead, the band would all assemble in a room, jam a lot and then hammer the best of what they came up with into some sort of shape. 'Creative,' yes. 'Controlled,' no.

Bassist Roger Glover explained that what they really wanted was a virtuoso, someone with the talent and drive to take them forward. They were not looking for a straight Blackmore replacement. Satriani had demonstrated that the guitar slot could be filled by someone with his own identity and style to very happy effect. Morse met the criterion. But what did he stand to gain? One answer would seem obvious: exposure and financial security. This was a difficult time for him personally, as he explained: 'I had a great upheaval in my life right as I joined the band with the divorce and stuff like that.'[110]

The public records for Florida record that Steven J. Morse was legally separated from Celeste Morse in 1995. Becoming part of a bigger organisation, the running of which was someone else's problem, may well have appealed to him at that moment.

When approached by Purple, his only question was, 'Is there a dress code?' It was not out of character. He later rationalised it as meaning, 'would he and the band be musically compatible?' He had never been to any of their concerts because they were not, at that time, playing much in the States and so he had little idea of their current sound, or what they were like live. This may have been his thinking, but given Morse's history, the phrase 'dress code' may have simply meant 'dress code'.

Morse met Glover at a club called Ziggy's in Winston-Salem, North Carolina, Glover having attended a Dixie Dregs gig. Morse agreed to jam with the whole band to see whether there really was any chemistry. To prepare, he listened to tapes of Blackmore and Satriani playing the band's repertoire live; of the two, he found himself taking a lot of his ideas from the latter. The session, when it happened, went well.

Morse said of it: 'We did a trial period and after the first, I'd say, hour everyone was smiling and we had instant communication.'[111] A picture of Morse with Glover, taken at that initial informal meeting, was hastily photoshopped to include the other members of the band and released as the first publicity shot for this latest Deep Purple line-up, or 'mark.'

Morse's debut appearance with his new colleagues took place in Mexico City on 23rd November 1994. It was preceded by three days of rehearsals. Colin Hart was tasked with collecting Morse from the airport: 'I had never met Steve until I went to pick him up in Mexico City for the first live rehearsal with us. He had been sent tapes from Roger. I asked if he'd like to go to the hotel and rest up, but he said no, and wanted to go straight to the rehearsal room.'[112]

As for Morse's contribution: 'He was amazing. He almost ran through the whole show at that first rehearsal like he'd been there for days! He was very easy to work with and pretty much just went with the flow.'[113]

Comparing him to the man he replaced, Hart said, 'A totally different player than Ritchie Blackmore. Both had their styles of play, but Steve adapted well to fit his style into the Purple playlist. As a colleague, he was a dream compared to Blackmore. Always on time, no pranks, no tantrums. He has a great sense of humour though!'[114] Hart qualified this somewhat with: 'Of course, that is not to say I didn't enjoy all my years with Ritchie Blackmore.'[115]

It is apposite to mention this comparison here because it would be a theme of Morse's tenure with the band, as Satriani had gloomily predicted.

If Morse believed that his time with Kansas — another band with a proud seventies-set history — was any kind of dry run for joining Purple, he was almost immediately disabused of the notion. He was now riding a juggernaut — less a band than its own micro-culture, one demanding almost total devotion. Almost.

They toured for around six to eight months in any given year — gruelling but still leaving time for side projects. Morse was a strong advocate of these: 'I think it's absolutely a necessity. With a band, out of necessity, you end up with a repetition when you are doing a tour and musicians can only stand so much repetition.'[116]

He almost immediately lived up to this by releasing a solo album, or a Steve Morse Band album, anyway, making it, strangely, his first studio output since joining Purple. *Structural Damage* is very heavy in places (the influence of his new employers, perhaps?), but otherwise showcases a familiar style. Morse made no apologies for this: 'You can't say goodbye to your style. Style mainly consists of repetition of certain elements, though I try to avoid repetition as much as possible.'[117]

The question for fans was whether Morse's style would clash with Deep Purple's. The signs were good, Glover rapturously praising Morse's creativity, talking up the sheer quantity of ideas that he brought to the table. Of these, Morse was clear that Purple could use the ones that they liked and that fitted their approach, but that he would have first claim on any others that might more readily suit his solo efforts.

He need not have worried: any jitters about compatibility were quickly assuaged. 'Eventually everything turned out to happen very naturally,' he said, '[drummer] Ian Paice jammed on a beat he liked, most of the times I could come up with something to play along, Jon and Roger filled that on, and Ian Gillan made the lyrics. This was the most natural way of composing I ever witnessed.'[118]

The process took up sessions that lasted from February to October 1995, with touring interspersed in between. The studio work was only a short distance from Morse's home, being based at Greg Rike Studios in Altamonte Springs, Florida. The same cannot be said for the tours, which visited such far-off destinations as Mumbai, India, for a gig that was filmed and recorded. Its setlist gave little away about the band's 'new' direction, being essentially the same as that from the last days of Blackmore, including what would prove to be one of the last ever live performances of Deep Purple's masterpiece, 'Child In Time.'

Only one new song was premiered, 'Purpendicular Waltz,' which is an enjoyable enough bash, but fairly standard issue. The only other clue came during the South Africa leg when members of the band (minus Gillan) did a radio interview, punctuating the chat with acoustic versions of some of the band's songs. One was a hitherto unheard piece called 'The Highland,' which would end up on the new album under a different title.

In March 1995, they all landed closer to Morse's home by making two 'secret' appearances at small venues in Orlando and Fort Lauderdale. In the event, they were not so secret: word spread on a new thing that had just emerged called the Internet, which would come to have a significant impact on the band, its fans, Morse and music as an art form and industry.

While all of this was going on, the Steve Morse Band managed a handful of gigs, mostly at US venues, although one at Van Gogh's Earlobe in Brisbane, Australia on September 8th stood out. A new album was also on the horizon, the uncompromisingly titled *Stressfest.*

It is an out-and-out rocker, even the quieter moments having a hard edge to them. The days of funky fusion were long in the past! Despite this, the recordings took place in the decidedly bucolic surroundings of the English Cotswolds. The album was released on 1st April 1996 and was well received by critics. *The Record's* review began: 'Steve Morse, late of Deep Purple, proves he has not lost any of his guitar wizardry on this fun-flavoured release.'[119]

It was pre-empted by the first Deep Purple album of the 'Morse era,' *Purpendicular,* which had come out in February. It was to become a favourite of Morse himself: 'I thought the album was really cool. I was envisioning how Jimmy Page would play guitar or acoustic. You'd also hear mandolins in some of Led Zeppelin's tunes. I thought Deep Purple's scope should be broader. So *Purpendicular* was an experiment that went, "Let's try anything that sounds good and see where we end up." For all those reasons, I love *Purpendicular.*'[120]

This comment references what is the album's most notable feature: its musical variety. It includes the expected heavy rockers, of course (with the addition of never before heard pinch harmonics!), but alongside them are the acoustic-led 'Sometimes I Feel Like Screaming', the poppy 'A Touch Away,' the funky 'Rosa's Cantina' and the folky 'The Aviator' — which was the final form of 'The Highland.' It would be an understatement to say that this was all a breath of fresh air after the numbingly formulaic *The Battle Rages On...*

The new guitarist's influence was felt not simply in the backings, but in the lyrics. 'The Aviator' is inspired by Morse's love of flying and recalls his notion that it is as much about the imagination as physical movement. Other songs are frequently focused on America and American ideas. Desert bars, blue collar strip clubs, Memphis and the gunslinger Johnny Ringo are all mentioned, as is a note written 'in perfect Spanish scrawl.'

Deep Purple had always been indebted to America to some extent: as, at bottom, a rock 'n' roll band, they played a genre that originated in the US and which was itself based on other genres from the US. This was, however, by far their most dedicated homage to the Land of the Free to date.

Glover argued that the success of the album was ultimately

attributable to the relationships between the people who made it: 'It's got nothing to do with the precision of the music or the playing or the quality of the songs or whatever. The atmosphere that's just in the studio somehow conveys itself.'[121]

That the album was a happy one to make was well attested by all involved. Of the writing process for it, Jon Lord said, 'While [Morse is] trying to remain his own man as a lead guitarist — which he has succeeded at, I believe — he's also tried to weave in some phrases and some ideas and some boogies and some feels that will make you feel like you are listening to Deep Purple.'[122] The question that this begs is, would the fans be convinced?

In terms of sales, *Purpendicular* certainly outperformed anything by the Dixie Dregs or Steve Morse Band but was still one of the lowest charting Deep Purple albums up to that point. Its unlovable predecessor had not done too well by that metric either but was still the more commercially successful of the two.

That the music was not precisely what the fans were expecting may have been a factor, as might the onset of fatigue around a band that had not been startlingly innovative of late. But the sad truth is that Blackmore had taken a substantial number of fans with him when he left. Morse tacitly acknowledged as much: 'All those people should just come to our show and listen. How can you judge such a thing without hearing it? And above that, the band is not the same as it was twenty-five years ago. I'm able to play Blackmore's parts, but I'm not him... On the front rows, there always those die-hards asking where Ritchie was. I don't bother with that at all, 'cause that's logical. He was one of the founders of this band. But at the end of the show, they'll know I play with just as much passion and energy as whoever else.'[123]

The frustration in this is palpable, but it evinces what would rapidly become an unalterable fact of life: the new era would not only be one in which the band would be forced to rebuild their fan base, but one in which Morse would have to prove himself. And not just once. Again and again and again...

9.
Fingers To The Bone

Morse's domestic life at this time was one of almost Waltons-like familial contentment. He was back to living on his farm and flying every day. He practised taekwondo with his son, which gave him a comprehensive daily workout. He also took up skateboarding, although the price of that was a broken wrist — not the most convenient injury for a guitarist.

Fans who were fortunate enough to score a backstage pass found themselves greeted by someone new, a friendly woman who had often been spotted selling 'merch' at Steve Morse Band gigs. Her name was Janine and she was Morse's new partner, later wife. From Van Nuys, California, and daughter to Emmet Boyce and Shirley Windsor, she was slightly younger than Morse, but still roughly his contemporary. Her background was something of a contrast to his, her West Coast sensibility leavening the no-nonsense Southern culture to which he had become accustomed. It was good for him: Morse was a home-loving man at heart and he could hardly have been more fortunate with how that side of things was going.

It was needed because his job was busy, almost frantically so. Much of 1996 was spent on the road promoting *Purpendicular*. Among the stops was the Montreux Jazz Festival. Whereas his first appearance there, way back in 1978, could just about be called 'jazz', this time that label was irrelevant, if not inappropriate. Of course, Montreux has something close to mythical status for Deep Purple fans. It was events in that town that had given the world the one non-negotiable entry on any setlist: 'Smoke On The Water.' Without realising it, or in any way meaning it, Morse was setting himself up for comparisons, flattering or otherwise, to be made.

Beyond such high points, the venues into which the band was booked were smaller than had been the case in the past. Where the

Blackmore-fortified line-up had regularly filled arenas, now sports halls and local theatres were more the order of the day — at least in European markets. More than anything this reflected nervousness on the part of the promoters: they simply had no idea whether the band were still a viable live act. How would the fans respond? Would there even be any fans? Happily, it proved to be something of a one-off experiment and future tours went back to being booked — mostly — in larger spaces.

The 1997 touring season got off to a memorable-for-the-wrong-reasons start with a concert at Estadio Santa Laura in Santiago de Chile on 27th February. It was to be an evening on which the constant carping from the Party of Blackmore would get to Morse, albeit in an atmosphere that was — to put it mildly — highly charged.[124]

Outside the venue, a crowd of people without tickets attempted to storm the turnstiles and had to be held off by water cannon-wielding police. Inside, just as the band were completing a version of the song, 'Into the Fire' (a fateful title if ever there was one), a large group climbed a lighting tower to get a better view of the stage. Being little more than a flimsy scaffold, the tower collapsed under their weight, landing straight on the heads of a portion of the audience.

Somehow, nobody was killed, but forty-four were injured, some seriously. The gig was suspended. Assuming it to be over altogether, the band left the stage and ensconced themselves in the minibus that was due to return them to their hotel. The promoters, fearing more trouble, not to mention a hefty financial loss, prevailed upon them to resume. The second half — considerably truncated — was a solemn affair and not one to remember.

It was further marked by a member of the crowd — one of the 'front row die-hards' no doubt — spending its entirety ribbing, flipping the bird at and spitting on Morse, one gob landing in Morse's mouth. Not unnaturally, he did not take kindly to this and, as soon as he finished playing, jumped down from the stage to remonstrate with his tormenter. Only the quick thinking of some handily placed stewards prevented matters from becoming physical. Morse later suggested that the incident helped to improve his image among fans who wrongly assumed that he was stage diving into them out of love and respect!

In reality, it stands out for revealing a side to Morse's character not often seen (or, for that matter, ever seen). Anger is not an emotion that seems to come easily to him. Yet, here he was on the verge of a fight in a very public place. In mitigation, it can be said that anyone would have felt on edge that night and he can hardly be blamed if the tension got to him. But it is an illustration — admittedly, an unusually graphic illustration — of the treatment that he received and continued to receive. For some, Blackmore was irreplaceable (despite his having been replaced twice in the past, by Satriani and, before him — a long time before him — by Tommy Bolin).

The whole, rather unnecessary, debate was a distraction, but there was plenty going on to take Morse's mind off it. The South American tour (which continued in trouble-free fashion) wound down in March, so that a new album could be recorded. This amounted to — pun intended — a purple patch for the band, who had been averaging an album every three years or so since the reunion in 1984. To record two almost back-to-back perhaps indicates just how much creativity Morse brought to the party — he, after all, had been close to an album-a-year man for much of his career.

The first sessions took place in June, with Lord largely absent because of his ongoing *Pictured Within* solo project. Whatever progress was made, the band were forced to reconvene (in Florida) in September to continue work.

There was a further interruption in the form of a tour of House of Blues clubs in the US. An investment by such diverse partners as Dan Aykroyd and Harvard University, House of Blues was a chain of restaurants-cum-live venues that has often played host to big name stars, attracted by the Hollywood connections. It was an opportunity to remind American audiences who Deep Purple were and perhaps cash-in on the new member's homeland appeal, although that was still very much to be filed under 'selective.'

A legacy of the tour was the reintroduction into the live set of a song that Morse had first encountered many years earlier — 'Hush.' The band's biggest ever hit in America, it had largely been ignored live since the late 60s because it belonged to the first iteration of the band, which did not include Gillan and Glover.

Famously, Gillan was generally against performing material that he had not co-written (although the band that he had fronted during Deep Purple's pre-1984 hiatus had achieved some chart success with cover versions).

Morse's — very sound — reasoning was that American audiences would not recognise much of the band's setlist but would possibly be familiar with 'Hush.' As he put it, 'I said, "What? How can you guys be playing a gig without doing 'Hush'? It just doesn't seem right!" And so I kept on and kept on it — kept on and kept on — and, finally, the band agreed to do it even! And it was the first time that Ian Gillan would be ever singing a tune of a Purple that he hadn't recorded originally.'[125]

Morse's Purple history knowledge isn't correct here. The band with Gillan had recorded a version of 'Hush' in the late 80s, and it had been included on the twenty-fifth anniversary tour of '93, with both Blackmore and Satriani but the point holds — and the song has never been dropped since.

'Hush' aside, the setlist erred on the side of the conservative. *Purpendicular* tracks were already quietly vanishing and within a year or two would be gone altogether, with few reappearances since.

From Morse's perspective it must have been more than a little irksome. Used to performing his own material, he was now — on the road, at least — a glorified contract player. He might well have tried to stamp his own personality on the songs, but they were still other peoples' songs. There is no significant documentary evidence of his having complained about it, but it would be understandable if he had felt that his contribution was not as central as it had been in his own bands.

Recording sessions for the new album dragged on into February of 1998, the result, *Abandon*, or 'A Band On,' finally seeing the light of day in May. As a collection, it is blisteringly heavy, the heaviest that the band had been in years and heavier than they would ever be again.

From the opener, 'Any Fule Kno That,' on, it rarely lets up. Even the more ballad-like numbers are uncompromising. The sole chink of lightness, 'Fingers to the Bone,' includes acoustic twiddling and a delightful piano break, but its spine is still some tough power chords.

Reviews were generally negative. Fairly typical was that from the UK's *Birmingham Post*: 'New guitarist Steve Morse brings some folky influences and nimble acoustic guitar work on high point "Fingers To The Bone" which is closer to the AOR of Asia or Foreigner than the hard riffing Deep Purple of old. A good thing, too, as it makes a pleasant diversion from the stentorian heavy rock that clogs up much of the remainder of the album.'[126]

Morse's view was, as should be expected, more upbeat: 'The opening track of *Abandon* — I love that. [I like] the fact that on *Purpendicular* they let me throw in some weird stuff like "The Aviator," and I always thought that Deep Purple could benefit from acoustic influence, like Jimmy Page did with Zeppelin.'[127]

Although the album was a commercial dud, the esteem in which it is held has grown over the years and it certainly still sounds very fresh. In the end, though, it has made even less impression on the live set than its predecessor. Beyond supplying material for the tours promoting it, it has been largely — well, what other word is there? — abandoned.

Of those tours, the pace was merciless and the stories legion. Morse has spoken of how an open-air gig in South Korea turned into a disaster as monsoon-like sideways lashing rain steadily destroyed a whole truck's worth of expensive equipment. Something similar happened in Switzerland, although this time, snow was the culprit. Supposedly, the temperature was so low that the musicians could barely feel their fingers. It is to be wondered what sort of show the paying punters enjoyed. A gig in Melbourne, Australia, was recorded and released later as *Total Abandon*, one of the band's best live albums.

As if being on the road with Deep Purple was not enough, Morse's workaholic nature got the better of him and he filled an empty August with a series of Dixie Dregs dates at Los Angeles' Roxy Theatre. The line-up was a sort of Dregs supergroup with all the original members taking part (Morse, Lavitz, Morgenstein, Sloan and West) as well as Goodman and LaRue. The core collective had not played together for nearly two decades, making this a particularly special occasion. The set list was packed with the band's classics as well as some astutely selected covers; a permanent record of the residency was released some time later as *California Screamin'*.

By this stage, the Dregs had morphed into an occasional diversion for its members, all of whom had other things to keep them occupied. This was certainly Morse's view; he was determined not to become sucked into the role of show runner again but found reunions fun for what they were: 'I enjoyed playing with the guys and by the time we got back together, a lot had been learned by everybody, and so it was more enjoyable.'[128]

As for Deep Purple, no new material emerged for a while, because they were about to become caught up in a project that would require all of their energy. For Morse, it would engage his eclectic side, but it was not to be the marriage of rock and jazz over which he had previously officiated. It would be an even more unlikely union of rock and classical.

For context, it should be said, that, while many see the album-for-the-ages that is *In Rock* as the debut Deep Purple output from the Gillan-fronted line-up, it was pre-empted, fact fans, by a live album with the intriguing title *Concerto for Group and Orchestra*. This was a record of the first and, for many years, only complete performance of an intensely experimental piece, composed by Jon Lord, that had been a deliberate effort to combine two genres that superficially had little in common.

It was thus not a series of songs by the band with an orchestra playing in the background; occasionally, the two units played together, for sure, but, in the main, they were kept apart, performing specially composed sections.

Morse gave an apt description of it: 'Bands like Metallica have done the orchestra thing. But the difference is they used it to sweeten the songs and make them fuller. With the "Concerto", the band is backing the orchestra up and coming in and out at different times.'[129] At nearly an hour in length, the 'Concerto' is a serious work and undoubtedly its composer's masterpiece.

The year 1999 would be its thirtieth anniversary and various members of the band — surprisingly, not Lord himself — began to moot the possibility of a revival. The problem was that no scores survived. The conductor Paul Mann, nephew of Colin Hart and a Lord family friend, speculated that they had been thrown out when the band's office was closed down in the dim and distant past. Transcribing the score from recordings and a film of the first performance was a possibility, but Lord was as committed to the Deep Purple touring schedule as anyone and simply did not have the time. Fortunately, a young man from the Netherlands named Marco de Goeij took it upon himself to do the necessary labour and suddenly a new version of the 'Concerto' went from pipe dream to reality.

The original performance — in 1969 — had been at London's Royal Albert Hall, so that was booked again, along with the London

Symphony Orchestra and Paul Mann. Morse has said that he was enthusiastic, based more than anything else on his respect for the composer: 'I'm one of Jon's biggest fans. I connected with him very intensely, especially on our first album, *Purpendicular*. He just had this certain something: he could hear things that no one else could.'[130] Of the 'Concerto' he said that it was the biggest production he had ever seen and that to, 'Hear Jon's work and be a part of it was absolutely incredible.'[131]

The plan was not to recreate the original programme precisely. That had been relatively stripped back: a couple of pieces by the conductor Sir Malcolm Arnold, a short set by Deep Purple, the 'Concerto' and an encore of one of its movements. End. It featured the band with the Royal Philharmonic Orchestra and no one else.

This time, the evening was to be a longer and more expansive celebration of the whole Deep Purple family. Each band member got a brief 'solo' slot, with invited guests helping out. For Glover, this meant enlisting the singer Ronnie James Dio to dust off a couple of songs from his *Butterfly Ball* project; Gillan raided the back catalogue from his own solo career and Lord focused on *Pictured Within* with vocals by Miller Anderson and Sam Brown. Ian Paice played the Deep Purple instrumental piece 'Wring That Neck' as a brassy big band jazz number.

Morse's slot took him all the way back to Dixie Dregs for his music and the Steve Morse band for his support. Joined on stage by LaRue and Romaine, he treated the audience to versions of 'Take It Off The Top' and 'Night Meets Light.' Both were well received, but more intriguing was what he did with the guitar parts from the 'Concerto.'

He has described his approach to the band's older material thus: 'On a tune that I didn't write, like "Smoke On The Water," I try to tread a line between homage and respect and originality. So, say, on the solo, I take it out a little bit and do it my way for a little bit and then bring it back to more like the original and wrap it up with a lick that everybody would recognise.'[132]

This was a philosophy that he carried into the Royal Albert Hall. On the First Movement, for example, Blackmore — in 1969 — essayed his parts as a continuous solo, some moments of which just happened to sound a bit like a riff. Morse, by contrast, upped the fuzzbox distortion to create a stronger sense of riff followed by a solo. The original sounds horribly dated now — definitely a product of the 60s — but the revival is a wall of sound, an unashamed chunk of heavy rock.

The section is shorter than it was, adding a feeling of tightness and precision. Morse changes the solo to suit his own style. This is something that is, perhaps, not often appreciated about the 'Concerto': Lord is credited as sole composer (with lyrics by Gillan), but the band's sections are mostly improvised, which argues for the piece as an artistic output being far more collaborative.

The first of the two performances was attended by a rowdy crowd, some members of which decided to interrupt the orchestral sections with repeated calls for the band's classic songs. Mann explained how this came about: 'Some people had seen the posters outside the Albert Hall and went, oh look, Deep Purple, with a symphony orchestra. Then when they found out that they had to sit there quietly, listening to music, you know, played by an orchestra, their expectations were obviously not fulfilled.'[133]

It was a problem that did not go away readily, but it was another example — which cannot have escaped Morse's attention — of how Deep Purple fans are not easy to please.

The band — and Morse — were not finished with the 'Concerto' as yet, but the grind of tours continued. The new year, the start of a new century and a new millennium was marked by another appearance at the Montreux Jazz Festival. This one was notable for including in the setlist a song that had literally only been composed at the sound check on the afternoon of the gig — 'Long Time Gone.' An enjoyably laid-back shuffle, its existence is testimony to the creativity of the band with Morse but its title was apt since it has never been heard of since. It was a reminder, however, that 'Abandon' was receding into the past and, a few mumbles about recording something 'soon' aside, a follow-up was not on the radar.

Ever the moonlighter, Morse was able to slip in another Steve Morse Band release while all of this was going on. *Major Impacts* was his homage to his influences, the tracks all being vaguely in the style of one or other of the many musicians or groups who had in some way shaped his sound over the years. 'Well I Have,' for example, is a nod to Jimi Hendrix, while 'Led On' has more than a hint of Jimmy Page about it. Other artists whose work is alluded to include Eric Clapton, The Byrds, The Allman Brothers, Kansas and Yes.

Morse summed up his process by stating: 'The challenges were there — like trying to give the impression of a guitarist in a vocal band with an original piece of music that doesn't use lyrics. And what are the components of a style? How to reflect those without actually repeating myself? The solution was to use familiar tempos, phrasing, instrumentation, and reminiscent themes that would be literally original but obviously intended to imitate.'[134]

With LaRue and Romaine once again as his wingmen, Morse created a hugely entertaining album that does its job with aplomb. A review in *The Daily Progress* mentioned his 'inexplicable tenure as guitarist with Deep Purple' before giving guarded approval: 'Dazzling playing abounds — the album is a showcase for Morse's versatility and dexterity — and the homages are, for any rock fan, tantamount to a clever round of hide-and-seek. Two and a half stars out of four.'[135]

The window for touring was narrow and the Steve Morse Band only managed a few gigs on the East Coast of the US in 2000, none of which featured songs from the album. The reason for this relative inactivity was simple — the band of which Morse was 'inexplicably' a member was calling, with one of their most ambitious requests yet.

In September a tour of the 'Concerto' hit the road, taking in South America before decamping to Europe. In fact, it was not just a Deep Purple tour with a jobbing orchestra attached but the whole Albert Hall shebang, with solo spotlights, guests — the works. Mann spoke of how this came about: 'It was actually at the Albert Hall after the second show: we were sitting in the bar backstage at the Albert Hall and someone said, wouldn't it be... we should tour this, we should take this out. And of course, [the band's manager] Bruce Payne was there and I remember him looking, really, are you serious? You know how complicated this is, how expensive this is — it's ridiculous! No chance!'[136] The rest of the world took a different view and offers to recreate the Albert Hall experience elsewhere led to a softening of this stance.

The first performance took place in Luna Park, Buenos Aires. As at the Royal Albert Hall, a vocal minority of the crowd saw fit to disrupt the more overtly classical sections. So bad did the heckling become that Mann was obliged to demand silence before beginning one of the movements. While such behaviour was not repeated everywhere, it was a leitmotif of the tour as a whole.

Mann put it down in part to the presence of Ronnie Dio, whose segment was longer than it had been at the London concerts and who had a sizeable following of his own. Since his music was straightforwardly heavy metal in style, his fans were likely to be even less forgiving of orchestral work than their Deep Purple counterparts, who were at least used to their favourite band going off in experimental directions now and then.

The European leg thus dropped many of the solo showcases and reverted to something much closer to a conventional Deep Purple gig with added 'Concerto.' Several old classic songs made a comeback. Turnout at the concerts was impressive, but planned stops in the US were shelved. A reprise came in the form of an orchestra-free Australian tour being temporarily suspended to allow for a performance of the 'Concerto' in Tokyo.

It was not to be Morse's last classical crossover. Believing that the band were some weird hybrid of high and low culture, Luciano Pavarotti of Three Tenors fame got in touch and invited them to perform at the 2001 iteration of his '...and Friends' charity concerts.

Arguably, the Italian maestro was an ideal collaborator with Morse. Both were classically trained (although if the rumours were true, Pavarotti never learned to read music) and both had histories of combining different genres. Morse's approach was well summarised by LaRue, who, surprisingly, dismissed the idea that he was principally a jazz musician: 'He isn't coming from that point of view. He's more influenced by straight ahead rock 'n' roll. He's got a Zeppelin and Hendrix background and he's influenced by bluegrass and classical music. A lot of his compositions are very classically orientated.'[137]

For their part, The Three Tenors (Pavarotti, Jose Carreras and Placido Domingo) — who were brought together in rather an ad hoc fashion to top and tail the Italia 90 World Cup competition with a little operatic bombast — virtually invented the genre known variously as 'popera' or 'stadium classical.' Essentially, this involved taking some of the catchier arias from operas and repackaging them as wave-your-lighter-in-the-air anthems. It was not fusion in the strict sense of the word but certainly lived in the same neighbourhood.

Pavarotti became closely associated with 'Nessun Dorma' (from Puccini's *Turandot*) which was a huge hit after being used as the theme tune to the BBC's coverage of the tournament. It was his signature song, his 'Smoke On The Water,' but he complained that he had none of the freedom of a rock singer to change the way that he performed it — any deviation from the score would have been swiftly punished by a vehement mob of critics.

The televised *Pavarotti and Friends* special in 2001 was held in the imposing surroundings of the Parco Novi Sad in the host's home city of Modena. The cast list was starry, featuring Barry White, Tom Jones, Anastacia and Morcheeba, with Michael Douglas and Catherine Zeta-Jones adding Hollywood cred and Donatella Versace bringing the cool.

Deep Purple made two interventions: inevitably, the first was 'Smoke On The Water'; improbably, the second was 'Nessun Dorma,' Gillan duetting with Pavarotti and thus starting something of a mutual admiration society that would last until the tenor's death in 2007.

So successful was Deep Purple's appearance that they were invited back to do it all again in 2003. It was a lovely distraction; whether Blackmore would have readily gone for it is something of an imponderable, but Morse was always game for new experiences and offered no objection. It was, if nothing else, time out from the band's punishing touring schedule, which, in early 2001, had them travelling around the US on a triple bill with Ted Nugent and Lynyrd Skynyrd (although that band was, by now, not much more than a tribute act).

It had been a whirlwind couple of years since the release of *Abandon* and much had been accomplished. Morse had embedded himself into Deep Purple quite effectively, although he would never fully be accepted by some, and the band had embarked on adventures that would probably not have been contemplated during the Blackmore dispensation. But there was little prospect of any new recording taking place any time soon and it was a matter of some dispute whether the Morse era had yet produced any out and out barnstormer tracks. As for Morse's side projects, they were trundling along nicely but had not really been boosted by his membership of one of the rock world's great behemoths. Still, new year, new century; all of that could easily change...

10.
Structural Damage

As *Major Impacts* eloquently demonstrated, Morse had many influences. Excluding the big ones — the Mahavishnu Orchestra and the like — he admitted to his sound including the fossils of many another band or musician. A good question, though, would be, 'who did he influence?' He had, after all, been in the business for a quarter of a century by the time he lined up on stage with Pavarotti and Friends for a night of borderline cringe fundraising. Who would have claimed to be a disciple of Morse?

It is an enquiry worth making. With his run of 'best of the year' behind him and Grammy nomination after Grammy nomination to his credit (no actual wins, but so what — a nomination is still an elevation to the elite), not to mention more excellent reviews than could easily be counted, why would he not have accumulated a small army of emulators?

The problem with finding an answer is that the obvious counter-question would be, 'which Morse would they emulate?' Would it be Morse the jazz fusionist? Morse the heavy rocker? Morse the player of acoustic classical pieces? How about Morse the bluegrass country boy? Imitating his eclecticism on its own would not really count, but even that concession does not suggest many viable candidates.

The truth is that he did not have a large following of practitioners. In proposing explanations, low sales cannot be discounted: it is hard to be influenced by someone whose music you have never heard. But, equally, the very variety of his playing may also have been a factor. He was quite simply too good to copy. It all goes back to style and Morse's deserved the over-used descriptor 'inimitable.'

An area upon which he could have been expected to have a bearing was the songs of the bands of which he was a part. From the pre-existing bands that he joined, the report card was, at this point in the narrative, none too inspiring.

The only real influence on his Kansas albums was MTV. Morse's distinctive voice was nowhere to be heard. As for Deep Purple, he could plausibly claim that *Purpendicular* was very much a Morse album. With its broad sonic palette, both in terms of style and technique, it was something new and unexpected. Yes, it had a few bangers, but the overall feel was light, complex. That was not so much the case with *Abandon*, which was a massive improvement on the execrable *The Battle Rages On...* but could still have been a Blackmore product. Heavy, intense and not overloaded with subtleties, it was a step back from what had been so recently achieved.

As for his own projects, The Dixie Dregs and Steve Morse Band were obviously going to reflect his tastes. He entered the new millennium, then, a man trapped between two worlds. This could be one interpretation of the title of his 2002 Steve Morse Band album, *Split Decision*. In fact, that is not the intended meaning; rather, it refers to mood, tempo and melody. The first half is tough rocking stuff, which eases back into some more classically-hued acoustic work in the latter stages.

Tracks such as 'Mechanical Frenzy' and 'Gentle Flower, Hidden Beast' provide the shredding bombast; the mellower cuts include 'Moment's Comfort' and the Bach-tinged 'Busybodies.' In his review for *pop matters.com*, Marshall Bowden says of the album, 'Listeners willing to flow along with the Steve Morse Band's creative inspiration will be well rewarded with a musical, yet rocking, experience.'[138]

Morse was pleased with what he and his band mates had created: 'I really enjoy the variety that doing solo projects gives me, and the *Split Decision* album, I think it has got the most breadth of different material that I've done in a really long time — and I think listening-wise it's easy to grasp for an instrumental thing. It's one of those albums, that the more you listen to, the more details and things you can find, because there was a lot of work that went into it, opposed to let's just go into the studio, and record, and be done by Friday.'[139]

If Morse's influence on the sound of Deep Purple had tended, so far, to fluctuate, something was about to happen that would swing the balance more in his favour: in September of 2002, Jon Lord left. It was far from a sudden decision. Gillan had said only half-jokingly that Lord had been halfway out of the door since 1998 and that, indeed, the band's failure to produce any fresh recorded material was the consequence — post-rationalisation if ever there was any. Lord himself explained that the success of the 'Concerto' extravaganzas and subsequent tours had convinced him to take a step that he had been thinking about for a long time - to try his luck as a full-on classical composer.

His initial thought was to take a sabbatical and he wrote to the band's management requesting a year off. When this was roundly rebuffed, he tendered his resignation. It was a civilised parting of the ways. Lord's last live appearances were on a guest basis, playing on a few tracks under the sufferance of his replacement, Don Airey. His last ever evening as a member of Deep Purple was passed at the Regent Theatre in Ipswich in the East of England. Afterwards, he stayed up all night with Paul Mann talking about the future. No doubt he veered between excitement and apprehension. He had, after all, been a member of the band since it started in 1968 — since before it started. It was his band.

Or, it had been. For Morse, Lord's departure had a number of repercussions. To start with, he lost a colleague he greatly admired. Not much research is needed to find interviews in which Morse waxes lyrical about Lord's wonderful ear and, especially, how it contributed to his own creativity. On the other hand, he was now the senior lead player in the band. And he had a willing ally in Airey.

Morse has said of him, 'Don and I work on ideas constantly. He is inclined to have an idea immediately about which way something should go — as am I. If these don't align perfectly, it's like, of course we could do it your way, or we could also do it the right way, which is my way. And there's more than one way. So sometimes we get into a little bit of disagreement about which way it should be but it's just because we're both enthusiastic and forthcoming with ideas very quickly.'[140]

Some of this creativity was evident in gigs from this time, which began to include a couple of yet to be recorded numbers: a Dregs-style instrumental, written by Morse, called 'The Well-Dressed Guitar' and a song, 'Up The Wall.' These were tentative first steps, but a new album could now justly be placed in the category 'coming soonish.' Promised recording sessions, however, had not occurred and the date by which new material would 'definitely' be available slipped several times. Discipline needed to be imposed.

This meant calling in a producer. Morse was used to working

that way and, indeed, had lauded the contributions that producers had made to his outputs, but it was a bold step for Deep Purple. They had used engineers in the past — most notably, the rock legend that was Martin Birch — but aside from the pre-Gillan and Glover days of the late 60s, when Derek Lawrence had overseen the first three albums, the albums since the reunion had been credited as produced by Roger Glover and Deep Purple, with the exception of *The Battle Rages On...* where Thom Panunzio, who had previously worked with the likes of Bruce Springsteen and Joan Jett had been brought in.

The man chosen this time was Michael Bradford, who had an excellent track record of working with Kid Rock, Madonna and many others. He was recruited by Brian Rawlings, an executive with Disney Music, who acted as what Bradford described as a 'matchmaker.'

Like Bob Ezrin, Bradford was a man who knew his own mind and was not afraid to stand up to the band's members in defence of what he saw as a good idea. Morse appreciated this, saying, 'He'll go ahead, listen to the versions and be polite, but he'll eventually say no, this is the way it should go and everybody wants that after so many albums of committee.'[141]

This manifested itself not only in vetoes of band members' ideas, but a large, if not dominant, role in the writing. The songs were heavily rehearsed and supposedly perfected. One consequence of this was a redraft of 'Up The Wall,' which was developed into 'I Got Your Number.'

The resulting album was released in August 2003 and went under the unenticing name *Bananas*. This had been proposed by Glover as a joke, only for him to find himself being taken seriously — no doubt to his consternation. As a piece of work, it has not aged well, although it received some good reviews on its release. John Benson, in the *News Journal*, gave it a guarded thumbs up before concluding: 'The band's new material is overshadowed by their heavy metal past, leaving most fans wondering when the next greatest hits tour will come through their town.'[142]

The *Florida Today* review was resoundingly positive, stating: 'The metal kings are back with their best album since 1984's *Perfect Strangers*, one that blends Deep Purple's power chords and banshee vocals with the memorable melodic hooks that earned the band a place in rock history.'[143]

Two of the tracks, 'House Of Pain' and 'Walk On,' are credited to Gillan and Bradford alone. Since Gillan's role has always been to write the lyrics, it can be assumed that Bradford was solely responsible for the music, cutting out the rest of the band entirely. Morse described how this happened, 'Michael said, "No, I want to do a more commercial tune and I'm going to bring it in and you guys are going to make it sound like you" and change the guitar riffs or whatever.'[144]

Another track, the soul-flecked, 'Haunted,' features backing vocals by Beth Hart. It was not unknown for the band to use other musicians — only recently, they had added an orchestra to large sections of their repertoire — but this was regarded as a controversial development that was hotly debated in Internet chat rooms.

The album's final track is a brief, typically classy, instrumental by Morse called 'Contact Lost.' He composed it upon hearing that Kalpana Chawla, one of the astronauts on the ill-fated Columbia Space Shuttle, had embarked on her final mission with some Deep Purple CDs in her bag, among them, *Purpendicular*. The tune's inclusion did entail the loss of 'The Well-Dressed Guitar', which was to be regretted.

Bananas did not sell in great numbers and is now not easy to source. There is a simple reason for this: the label, to all intents and purposes, deleted it. Gillan expressed his annoyance at this turn of events, 'EMI in the UK pressed — and sold easily — 18,000 copies. They refused point blank to produce any more.'[145]

This led, perhaps inevitably, to band and label parting company. They have not worked together since. In fact, EMI missed a trick because the whole falling out had been in part precipitated by their rejection of the recordings of the 'Concerto' revival, only for said recordings to be released by the newly established Eagle Rock, with a level of success that kept the fledgling label afloat.

Morse had other matters on his mind, not least his membership of a 'supergroup' called Living Loud, which, as much as it definitely qualified as a group was, in all honesty, only slightly 'super.' As is often the way in the fraught world of rock music, it resulted from an acrimonious falling out.

The impetus had come from bassist Bob Daisley and drummer Lee Kerslake, whose extensive resumes included contributing to Ozzy Osborne's hit releases *Blizzard Of Ozz* and *Diary Of A Madman* — which is where their problems began. Having sued Osborne for unpaid royalties, they discovered that the albums had been reissued with their parts replaced by performances from other musicians.

As co-writers of many of the songs, they were unwilling to take this lying down and resolved to record their own new versions, although Daisley gave a desire to pay tribute to the late Randy Rhoads — the guitarist who had played on the two Osborne albums — as a further motivation. Australia-based minor legend Jimmy Barnes was quickly recruited as vocalist, but Morse — the only choice for the lead instrument — was a more difficult fish to land.

Approached by executive producer Drew Thompson, who, in another guise, was closely associated with Deep Purple, Morse was reluctant at first because, 'The idea of recreating the Ozzy stuff without anything different wouldn't have been for me and, when I first heard that, I thought, "There are a lot of guitarists who can do that; great Drew, I'll talk to you later." And he said, "Wait! They'd like to do some material that's original." And that's more like me. When I was working with Bob and Lee, Bob was, "Yeah, let's try some different things." That's more my style because I can't help but change arrangements.'[146]

Daisley began by viewing Living Loud as a stand-alone project, each track featuring different guest stars. A little jamming with the core group put paid to that. As he said, if everything is going so well, why change anything? So, it turned into a band — or, anyway, a potential band. Morse was clear that it was only his side hustle: 'If Living Loud was playing a gig just before, opening for Deep Purple, I don't think the guys would like that at all. However, the fact that it's something occasional fits right in with Deep Purple very well because everyone in the band does that and it's encouraged and everyone says it makes a stronger band because the musicians are stronger.'[147]

The main recordings took place, conveniently for Morse, in Florida and the whole thing was done and dusted in a couple of weeks. Barnes suggested that this was because everyone was so talented that they did not need any longer, but it could also have been down to the difficulty of finding windows in otherwise packed schedules.

Morse pointed out that the recording period was not the be all and end all, 'That doesn't count the time we spent working on the songs, which is probably another ten or fifteen days and I wouldn't have minded if it had taken sixty days to record because I got a little bit rushed through the guitar parts.'[148]

The process started with the basic tracks being laid down by Morse, Daisley and Kerslake. Morse was comfortable with this since his own band had been a trio for years. He has spoken of appreciating how it simplified the writing process, there being fewer competing voices than in Deep Purple.

Barnes arrived some days later, sat down with a notepad and wrote lyrics where needed more or less on the spot. Morse found such working methods particularly fruitful: 'The four of us just sitting in my practice room here in Florida and we were working on the tunes so quickly. Like you could throw into the middle of this circle of people 120 years or so or maybe 150 years of experience. And that collective body of experience was awesome!'[149]

A final addition to the group was a certain Don Airey (who had also worked with Osborne in the past) although he did not involve himself with any writing and did not appear on every track: 'My part in it is very peripheral,' he said, 'I just came in for an afternoon. Bob phoned me up and said, "I'm in London. We've got Air Lyndhurst Studios. Would you come in and add a few overdubs for the album?" So that's what I did. I went in for six to seven hours. Bob and I spent most of the time laughing ourselves silly about the old days. I played on five or six tracks.'[150]

Six Osborne songs were covered, including 'Crazy Train' and 'Mr Crowley,' but the five originals are arguably more exciting. Hard-edged rock of the type that Deep Purple were quietly moving away from, they are all great fun and very catchy. 'Last Chance,' for example, sounds like Bon Scott-era AC/DC — not surprisingly perhaps given the Australian connection. Especially noteworthy is the single, 'In The Name Of God,' which is about the hypocrisy of religious people who talk of peace while endorsing, or engaging in, the killing of those who do not share their beliefs.

Daisley described its creation: 'The song came about at the end of our time of writing the stuff, which was really, really crammed with work, it was a short period of time — I think we were at Steve Morse's place in Florida for probably eight days, and in that eight days, we had to rearrange and write new parts for the Ozzy stuff and rehearse that stuff and write. First of all we'd written four more and then we said we need at least one more song to balance the ratio out of old stuff and new stuff. Steve started playing like a Spanish sort of thing. I said let's do more of an Eastern sort of thing. So, we worked the music out together first. Then Jimmy came up with the idea of 'In The Name Of God' because it sounded sort of Eastern and this was July 2003 and this Iraq thing was going on and we all know what that's all about.'[151]

UNICEF contacted Drew Thompson expressing interest in a song that so eloquently expressed their values. Or he contacted them. Either way, they adopted the song for promotional purposes, all royalties going to fund their work.

Perhaps predictably, reviews for the eponymously-named album were respectful-to-good, but sales barely registered, Barnes' status (at least, in Australia) notwithstanding. The presence of Morse and Airey did nothing to help it either. UNICEF, it can be assumed, did not make as much as they might have anticipated.

As an overall experience though, it was one that Morse enjoyed. He was keen to take the band on the road and there were some gigs in Australia (Airey being part of the line-up). Another studio album was hinted at, but, as to whether it would consist of entirely new material, Morse could only say: 'I'd imagine so. But you never know what Bob [Daisley's] thinking.'[152]

In the end, though, planned dates in Europe did not happen and the retirement of most participants, not to mention the sad passing of Kerslake in 2020, meant that Living Loud is destined to remain strictly a one-shot phenomenon. Apart from the album, a recording of a gig from Sydney is its only other legacy.

While publicising the band, Morse brought up an issue that had been on his mind before and which would grow in importance as the years went by: 'With a tour the overhead monster is so big that there's this mythical belief and I say mythical because I'm against this concept but the mythical belief is that you've got to play a certain number of gigs just to break even — you can't do it with just a short tour. One of my crusades with any band I'm in is to do a lot of short tours and pack them together and manage the business end of it very carefully so it can be done. I think bands are fresh and really explode on short tours.'[153]

He was not to get his wish — at least, not yet. Deep Purple's ceaseless trudging around the world continued. There were some highlights. A gig in Mexico City was preceded by the band being presented with the remains of the albums taken into space by Kalpana Chawla, together with a certificate of authentication from NASA. A trip to the USA saw the band reunite with Joe Satriani, who shared the bill: the post-Blackmore world embodied. But there was still no sign of any new studio material. And Living Loud was already in Morse's rear-view mirror.

Dixie Dregs 1981.
(Arista Records promotional photo)

With Dixie Dregs at the Fox
Theatre, Boulder, Colorado
USA, 16th June 1992.
© Bill O'Leary / Timeless Concert Images)

Along with the following two pages,
more shots from the Fox Theatre,
Boulder, Colorado USA, 16th June
1992. The band played two shows
that night, hence the different
clothing.

© Bill O'Leary / Timeless Concert Images

Back to the Fox Theatre in Boulder, the following year; 10th January 1993.

© Bill O'Leary / Timeless Concert Images

The first European tour with Deep Purple.
Brielpoort, Deinze, Belgium,
6th October 1996.
© Marc Brans

Backstage at Forest
Vorst National,
Brussels, Belgium,
24th September 1998.
© Marc Brans

2003, Nandrin.
© Marc Brans

With Deep Purple at the "Schwung 2004" classic rock festival at Roeselare Hallen in Belgium on 8th July 2004, where Purple headlined a bill that also included, Status Quo, Cheap Trick and UFO.
© Marc Brans

With Ian Gillan at London's O2 Arena, 17th November 2017. Morse had been with Deep Purple for over two decades by this time, and the band was having a renaissance with two very strong albums produced by Bob Ezrin, who Morse had previously worked with in Kansas.
© Jerry Bloom / Wymer (UK) Ltd

11.
Slice Of Time

Steve Morse was fifty. In previous ages, he would have long since hung up his Frankenstein Telecaster and knuckled down to bundling hay. He has described the farm as a big responsibility, his collection of tractors often needing repairs and maintenance. It can be imagined that, in some alternative universe, he took on that responsibility, settled down and became a full-time worker of the land. He might have kept his hand in musically by writing the odd song for other, younger, artists, perhaps even racking up a hit or two (he would go on to do this, but with the usual lack of chart impact). He could have made more money that way than he ever managed as a performer. Every so often, he could have got the Dregs back together for a benefit concert, or an anniversary tour (without straying too far from home).

But, even in 2004, the world had entered the Era of the Forever Rock Star and, for those who were older, careers began to fluctuate between two possibilities: calling it quits and an ever more infinitely deferred retirement. Even having reached his landmark birthday, Morse was still, by some distance, the youngest member of Deep Purple, which left the question of whether whatever they were doing at any given moment — recording an album, hitting the road, promoting something — would be for the last time. No one was yet talking about giving up, but the possibility was to become increasingly salient. For now, though, age was only a number and the pace of work never slackened.

Whether Morse was in a reflective mood is difficult to say. If he has come across as anything in the narrative so far, it has been as an optimist and lover of his art, as much as the business side of music might have pissed him off more often than not.

The title of *Major Impacts 2*, which came out in 2004 (credited to

Steve Morse alone), implied a taking stock, but it was just a sequel —
if the word can be used — to its non-numbered predecessor. Again,
it is a series of original pieces in the style of bands that influenced
Morse and, again, the voices of the influencers can be heard, but
they are not so loud as to drown out that of Morse himself. His
distinctive imprimatur — that 'style' of his own that does not change
— is on every track. The album is a fine listen, even if, commercially,
it remained strictly for connoisseurs.

If Morse needed reminding of the passing of the years, it came
from Deep Purple's involvement in Live 8, a series of concerts held
in July 2005 to commemorate the twentieth anniversary of the
zeitgeist-definer that had been Live Aid. Timed to coincide with a
G8 summit, the two concerts of the original were expanded to ten
covering all of the G8 countries along with South Africa.

The goal, too, was more ambitious. Whereas Live Aid had aimed
to raise funds for relief of a single famine, this time millionaire rock
stars gigged for no less a cause than to abolish poverty all around
the world. The roll call of talent was impressive — Madonna, U2,
Paul McCartney and a reunited — just — Pink Floyd all donated their
time. A-listers such as Brad Pitt and Will Smith were relegated to
the role of compères. Everywhere, the stars glittered.

Except at the Canada branch of the franchise, held in Ontario
and introduced by the decidedly underpowered Dan Aykroyd. To be
fair, the likes of Celine Dion, Mötley Crüe and Neil Young were not
exactly obscure, but they were not in the full flush of youth and no
doubt saw their involvement as a golden opportunity to gain a bit of
free publicity.

Deep Purple were programmed alongside them and were thus
implicated in the ridicule levelled at the event for being populated
by has-beens. The *Winnipeg Sun*, for example, wrote of it: 'Live 8
Canada is tragically un-hip. This is your mum and dad's rock concert,
just an Anne Murray away from Branson, Missouri. Where are the
acts from this century?'[154]

Morse's main story from the event concerned Ian Gillan walking
out on to the stage barefoot, only to run off to procure some shoes
having had his soles burned by the plastic flooring. The band played
'Smoke On The Water' (obviously), 'Highway Star' and 'Hush.' As
they came off, Gillan mouthed some platitudes to a reporter about
the importance of wiping out poverty before the band underlined

the point by taking a private jet to their next gig, which was to be held in Illinois.

Live 8 was not the only major moment for the band from 2005. Nor was it the only one that touched on the passage of time. Gillan realised that he had been in the music industry for forty years and that some form of commemoration was due. So, he made an album of re-recorded songs from most parts of his career under the title *Gillan's Inn*. Many of his erstwhile collaborators joined in to up the fun factor. Joe Satriani, Tony Iommi and Janick Gers were among those who took part, as were everyone from the current Deep Purple line-up.

Thus, Morse played a few familiar riffs, making his contribution from the comfort of his home studio before it was mixed with parts provided by others to produce the final selection. That in itself was a marker of history moving on: it would simply not have been possible when all of those involved started out on their rock journeys.

The year also saw Deep Purple recording a new album, *Rapture Of The Deep*, which was in the can by June. The label was Edel, from Germany. Michael Bradford returned as producer, but his role was radically different from what it had been on *Bananas*. Whereas he had been a central figure in that project, now he was kept strictly out of the limelight. He received no writing credits and was not featured in any publicity material. It is easy to not notice that he was involved at all.

The album and its production were very different from *Bananas*. That had been produced to within an inch of its life, meticulously rehearsed and multilayered. With *Rapture Of The Deep* interview after interview stressed its spontaneity. Glover, for example, said of it: 'We'd go in, write what was going to be the idea for the song and immediately go into record mode and capture it. Michael is very good at stopping us from overdoing it. Usually, it's two takes and that's it!'[155] The message was clear: we messed up last time, but now we're giving fans what they really want!

Unfortunately, that was not borne out by sales when the album was released on 24th October. They provided no justification for the Michael Jacksons of this world to start looking nervously over their shoulders.

In hindsight, the chief success of the album is that it defined a sound for this incarnation of the band that was sufficiently 'Deep

Purple' to keep the strong links to the past, but original enough to be a thing in and of itself.

Airey makes much greater use of synthesisers than Lord ever did, most notably in the solo for 'Back To Back.' Morse rarely sounds anything like a Blackmore clone. 'Wrong Man' has a throbbing riff that is all his own, while the dissonant, moody, Doors-alike 'Before Time Began' would have been unimaginable in any age prior to his joining. That, lyric wise, it echoes Living Loud's 'In The Name Of God' is probably pure coincidence.

Reviews were mixed. The spectacularly hard-to-please *Winnipeg Sun* gave one so damning and so brief that it can be quoted in full: 'Gillan, Paice and Glover are still around. The inspiration and brilliance, sadly, are long gone. For indiscriminate completists only.'[156] Happily, the BBC took a different line saying, more than slightly hyperbolically: 'This is classic Deep Purple. Welcome back!'[157]

Well... mmm... Classic Deep Purple? No. Good Deep Purple, yes. Promising Deep Purple, for sure. Not devoid of inspiration and brilliance, but not classic. There are standouts — some already mentioned as well as the title track, which survived on set lists for some years. But the song that had the most notable impact on live performances was not even included on most versions of the album.

'Things I Never Said' was added as a bonus exclusively for the Japanese market before sneaking out elsewhere as a B-side (if such a thing can still be said to exist). It was finally elevated to full album status as part of a special 'tour edition' that came out some months later and which, finally, included a studio take of 'The Well-Dressed Guitar' along with a few inessential 'extras.'

As Morse was engaged in all of this, somewhere in the background Phil Walden was losing a battle with cancer. He finally succumbed in April 2006. After a life lived at breakneck speed, such an end had a veneer of commonplace tragedy about it. Walden was robbed of the grand exit that he had earned.

Capricorn Records had already gone, its second coming ended by a lucrative sell-off in 2000. Walden ploughed the funds raised into yet another label, the less notorious Velocette which he ran as a Walden family affair. Some years later, in 2014, the building in Macon that had been the first home of Capricorn was condemned and razed to make way for new developments. A chapter had been brought to a definitive close.

Morse's life continued with *Rapture Of The Deep* making its faltering way in the world while he, Airey and Paice participated in another recording project, one so obscure that it is now difficult to find a reference to it anywhere — including the Internet. It can be purchased on iTunes but otherwise seems to have completely disappeared. Even AllMusic carries no review of it.

It is *E-thnik* by Mario Fasciano, an Italian singer and composer with a high-pitched voice who sang songs that hovered somewhere between folk and electronica. It is enjoyable enough, but to call it a curio would be to overstate its reach. It is doubtful that most fans of Morse or any of the bands of which he is a member have ever heard of it. Yet Morse and Paice (with Airey augmented by Rick Wakeman) did it all again in 2007 on the Fasciano offering *Porta San Gennaro Napoli*, the title of which suggests a live album, although it does not especially sound like one.

On both, Morse's acoustic lines drip class and technique, despite keyboards taking the main role. Considering he is so highly billed; Paice does nothing outside of his comfort zone and is barely there on some tracks. Perhaps the most significant part of *E-thnik* was that the punning title inadvertently touched on another side to Morse that was coming more to the fore at this time, a political side.

Of course, it would be wrong to deny that he had ever lacked any sort of political consciousness. He was, after all, the kid who marched for hair. But his music, outside of a couple of Deep Purple's milquetoast protest songs, had never really shown much engagement with broader societal issues.

Now, though, he added to his stage costume (which had always been more carefully curated than he had been prepared to admit) a Native American necktie. He explained the reasoning behind this: 'I have a typically mixed American heritage, predominantly European. So, I'm Caucasian,' and, he added, a patriotic American. However: 'I have been spiritually aligned with the Native Americans since I read about the history of the USA.'[158]

Was he conflicted, then? He was clear-eyed when it came to spotting injustices: 'I am more of a witness than anything else. I am a supporter of not forgetting the fact that we came here and unnecessarily took over more than we had to. People should be able to work together and live together. We didn't have to humiliate them, take everything from them and practically commit mass genocide against them.'[159]

He was being too modest in citing himself as nothing more than an interested observer. He played benefit concerts for various Native American causes. One such cause that had a particular effect on him, since it was he who brought it up in various interviews, concerned an old Navajo woman who faced eviction from her land.

Morse told the story: 'This nice elderly lady was raising sheep on that land. She spun wool and made dye from plants on that land to make things from the wool she spun. The government was going to move her and kick her off that land because they found some minerals in the ground. I really can't stand things like that and I had to help her because she was such a wonderful person: she is dead now.'[160]

This is not simply the voice of a caring outsider, but empathy from a son of the soil for a peer. Morse said that the old woman presented him with a Native American rug that she had made herself, shearing the wool, spinning it, weaving it, dying it. He added it to his collection of indigenous artefacts from around the world.

It is a pity that the old woman could not spin Deep Purple a new album because in the wake of *Rapture Of The Deep*, they entered a long period in which no new material was recorded, or even looked like it was going to be. Occasionally, one or other member of the band, usually Glover, would give an interview in which they would talk about getting back into the studio, sometimes even giving dates, but nothing came of it.

Excuses were made, but the truth is that there was no motivation to do any recording. None of the albums since *Purpendicular* had sold well, part of a general trend in the music industry. Morse bemoaned the situation, saying: 'All indications for anyone who isn't doing rap music, why bother recording? Why bother making free downloads?'[161]

He was being more than a little disingenuous. The quotation above continues with an affirmation of Deep Purple's commitment to songwriting and recording — and he did not shirk his duties in this regard in his activities beyond the band. He, for example, joined his old pals T. Lavitz and Jerry Goodman in School of the Arts, which released a self-titled album in 2007.

Essentially a vehicle for Lavitz, who composed all of the tracks, the band was another Mahavishnu Orchestra clone, combining guitars, keyboards and violin. The style was fusion, with an acoustic twist. The original concept was to banish electric instruments altogether, but this was modified slightly when it was found that an acoustic bass was more trouble than it was worth.

Later, Morse would claim that he appreciated not having to be a creative driving force and was happy to just do his thing and let Lavitz call the shots. That was a simple enough concession, because the album was another exercise in the application of technology, parts recorded in remote locations being cut and pasted into a final form later; Lavitz called it a 'jigsaw album.' In interviews, he lamented the loss of the kind of atmosphere that could be generated by all of the musicians occupying the same space at the same time. Intriguingly, he went on to issue an open invitation to Morse to pitch some song ideas that they could work on together.

Most reviews came from jazz-orientated publications. In general, the album was well-received, particular praise going to the relative lack of clashing egos it displayed, its collaborative nature earning plaudits. But it was a one-off. There were no gigs and no follow-up. Lavitz explained why: 'It's about scheduling. I didn't know how good [the album] would come out. I thought it would be good, but I never realised until it was done how good it was going to be. I really haven't been in touch with anybody. These guys travel so much, and they're going in three different directions.'[162] Soon enough, a follow-up became an impossibility.

Angelfire was another project that began to occupy Morse in 2007, although an album wasn't released until three years later. Essentially, a duo, it consisted of Morse and the singer Sarah Spencer. The two came together in a rather unconventional manner, as Morse related: 'That started when a friend, who's a guitar player and a doctor, said: "Can you give my family some advice? Our daughter wants to be a singer." I said, "I don't know. I've got to hear her sing, first." He brought over some recordings and I said, "Oh, she's got a great voice." Sarah's voice is a really pure voice that's not full of attitude. It's beautiful.'[163]

As much as this sounds like Spencer was living a fairy tale, it is not the whole story. She had, in fact, been experimenting with music since the age of eleven, trying her hand at different genres, including classical, a direction encouraged by her vocal trainer Shannon Riley.

She had performed live on many occasions and worked with various established musicians, such as Paul Weston, who became a regular co-writer.

Later, she was taken under the wing of Charlotte Church's vocal coach and even recorded a song for a Cinderella film (which, admittedly, fits well if the 'fairy tale' line is insisted upon...).

By the time she met Morse, then, she was not only something of a veteran (at the age of sixteen) but could fully sympathise with his love of mixing and matching styles and genres. Her view of the partnership was: 'Steve has been so generous throughout our collaboration. Everyone knows about his incredible talent, but only a lucky few know about his big heart. I feel so blessed to work with this Renaissance man!'[164]

Morse offered to work with her on some writing and recording, using his home studio. It proved to be a fruitful experience, both parties bringing much to the table. Of the division of labour, Spencer said: 'We co-wrote everything on the album together, but I mainly put down the lyrics, and Steve mainly did the music. Of course, there were times where we would both put down some lines, and one song on there ("Feelings are Overrated") was an old track of mine that Steve resurrected, so it wasn't split right down the middle, 50/50. But for the most part, Sarah = lyrics, Steve = musical genius, arrangement/production.'[165] Filling out the sound of the core pair were Morse's faithful retainers LaRue and Romaine. The former recorded his parts in Florida, but Romaine phoned his in from New York and Germany.

It was still some time before the recordings would see the light of day, but they are a reminder — if one were needed — that Deep Purple's raucous species of rock was only one side of Morse's musical personality. The *Angelfire* album is a delightful piece of acoustic new age minstrelsy, Spencer's voice having a charming artlessness that goes well with Morse's six string twiddling. Album standout 'Everything To Live For' is a good example of the overall style as well as, in its title, carrying a message for a rocker who was by now advancing through his fifties.

If Morse needed reminders of his mortality, it came with the deaths of several people close to him in quick succession. Most tragically, in 2007, his father passed on. In spite of his opposition to popular music, it is to be imagined that he was proud of his son's incredible achievements. Morse made sure that he was next to his father's bedside at the end.

Following that, two of Morse's old band mates also died. The first, in 2008, was Hiram Bullock. Two years later, it was the turn of T. Lavitz. The material that he hoped to produce with Morse remained a tantalising possibility only. The Angelfire album opened with a song called 'Far Gone Now.' It was a title that had haunting resonances at the time; it would acquire more and more in the years to come.

12.
Brave New World

The noughties were a strange time in Russia. The Soviet Union was a thing of the past and the reversion to authoritarianism that was to have such unfortunate consequences years later had not yet taken hold. Practices that had been clandestine in the past were out in the open, among them, listening to rock music. It had always been done, of course, but 'decadent' Western music had earned little favour from the Communist Party and being a fan of it was to court disaster. Many a youngster had been forced to defy the local commissariat by making secret copies of their favourite albums on that medium hallowed by people of a certain age, the C90 cassette.

One such youngster had been a certain Dmitry Medvedev, who had loved all of the big names from the period: Black Sabbath, Led Zeppelin, Pink Floyd and, it should go without saying, Deep Purple. In later life, as Russian president elect, he mobilised his influence in the cause of persuading Deep Purple to perform at a concert, held in the Kremlin, to celebrate the fifteenth anniversary of the state natural gas monopoly Gazprom (which is about as Russian a reason for holding a celebratory concert as can be imagined).

Medvedev came across as decidedly starstruck: 'I was thirteen or fourteen when I first listened to Deep Purple and such music was forbidden then. It would be completely surreal to imagine that I would meet this legendary band in the Kremlin — but it happened.'[166]

Gillan wrote about the event for the *Sunday Times*, noting that younger members of the audience seemed nervous, unsure as to precisely what level of enjoyment would be tolerated by bosses for whom Communist-era strictures were still a vivid memory. After the show, Medvedev and the chief executive of Gazprom joined the band in their dressing room for a few drinks and a chat. As subject matter, politics was studiously avoided.

It was an open secret that the version of the band that Medvedev had listened to as a teenager had not been the one that included Morse and Airey. What Morse thought about it all has trickled through in interviews here and there. His line was characteristically conciliatory: 'Medvedev's a music man! But it just goes to show you: everywhere you go, people are pretty much the same.'[167]

A month after the Gazprom concert, in March 2008, Medvedev lost the 'elect' bit to become actual President. He replaced Vladimir Putin, who had had to step down for constitutional reasons. Medvedev promptly appointed Putin Prime Minister, a post that was technically inferior, but, in reality... well... it is probably enough to say that it was occupied by Putin. But whatever else Medvedev achieved in his role, he was able to lure Deep Purple back for another meeting...

But there was much to be done before that occurred. There was, for example, a world record to break. On 1st May 2009, Morse joined 6,345 other guitar players — the largest guitar ensemble ever — at the 'Thanks Jimi Festival' in Wroclaw, Poland, to play the riff to 'Smoke On The Water,' followed by that of the Hendrix hit, 'Hey Joe.'

Most of the instruments used were acoustic, which not only would have kept the volume at a reasonable level but eased the burden on the local electricity supply. The feat having been accomplished, everyone held up their guitar to produce a view that Morse described as resembling a forest.

That having been done, a new Steve Morse Band album, *Out Standing In Their Field*, was released in September. Its title notwithstanding, to say that it breaks new ground would be to say far too much. It is what it is: virtuosic, entertaining, replete with riffs that would grace Deep Purple if Gillan could be persuaded to sing over them and a few punning titles that just about sidestep groan-inducing territory. All the usual influences are there, from metal in the opener, 'Name Dropping,' to baroque in, not surprisingly, 'Baroque 'N Dreams.'

Artistic qualities aside, *Out Standing In Their Field* is most fascinating for its timing. Morse had already alluded to the impact of music downloads at the time of Living Loud, but they were becoming ever more significant and were a major contributor to the inexorable decline of the album. Bundling together a number of tracks recorded at roughly the same time only makes sense with physical formats.

If tracks can be purchased from the Internet and stored on a device individually and at any moment in time, what need all the rigmarole that goes along with making, pressing and distributing an album?

In her review of *Out Standing In Their Field*, Emily Tuttle, praised it on the grounds that, 'When I listen to every song on a CD and don't want to skip tracks, I know I've got a keeper.'[168] She referenced a physical format, but her words apply doubly to downloads. Keeping impatient fingers off the 'next' button became a priority for those producing music.

Worse was the trend towards only downloading certain tracks: why pay for 100% of an album when only 30% of the tracks are desired? Just buy those tracks! Various methods were tried to forestall such an attitude: compilations that gathered 'unmissable' songs had always been popular, but they became more so.

Morse had put out his own in 2005 (*Prime Cuts*) that drew on his recordings for the label Magna Carta, the recent home of the Steve Morse Band. Live albums also began to appear in dizzying profusion. Deep Purple produced several, but others that featured Morse included Steve Morse Band's *Cruise Control* from 2008 and Kansas's *There's Know Place Like Home* from 2009. The aim of these was generally to recreate the concert experience in full, thus making the purchase of single tracks less attractive.

The year 2008 was further notable for the debut of an Internet platform that would prove a major challenge to working musicians struggling to make a decent living — Spotify. If anything has promoted what Alan Krueger has called the 'Bowiefication' of music — that is, the de-commodifying of it by making it ubiquitous and impossible to adequately monetise[169] — the trend of which Spotify (and, earlier, Napster) was in the vanguard was the start of it.

Morse expressed a willingness to embrace a new way of working: 'My vision was every [Deep Purple] tour we'd do another song and just release it on the web site. I'd say, "Don't even try to sell it, because things are different these days as far as how people listen to music."'[170]

For him, this was a very important matter because it was largely responsible not only for Deep Purple's continued reluctance to go into a studio but the long tours that he so disliked. The one fed into the other: a musician cannot be in a tour bus and in a recording studio at the same time (although Morse was often obliged to follow the tour bus in a car because his constant tinkering with his guitar became too much for his band mates to take).

Out Standing In Their Field kept the album as a form alive — at least for Morse. And Emily Tuttle liked it enough to listen to the whole thing. The *Angelfire* album, which finally appeared in 2010, was similar in that respect, if not in others. It did not, for example, give a sense of having the same impetus behind it. From any point of view, it was never going to make too many waves: it failed to get within a flight in Morse's plane of a decent placing on any chart.

It did amass some solid reviews. Spencer's voice — positioned somewhere between Patti Smith, Sarah McLachlan and Enya — received well-deserved plaudits. The relatively low-key Morse backing was also well regarded, although most critics lamented that there was not enough of it.

To promote the album, the duo sort-of hit the road in 2010, opening for Steve Morse Band. This meant that Morse supported himself on his own tour. Then again, the Steve Morse Band had habitually opened for Dixie Dregs, so he was well used to being both the main attraction and the also-ran on any given bill.

But, like Living Loud and School of the Arts before it, Angelfire proved a creative dead end. Unlike its predecessors, however, it does not seem to have been conceived as an ongoing project from the get-go. No follow up recordings ever happened or were even mooted as far as can be ascertained. The gigs were more to introduce the material and give Spencer some experience than to announce the presence of a new band. If they helped to shift a few copies of the album too, then so much the better.

Back in Deep Purple Land, the second meeting with Medvedev took place in 2011. This time, the band were not part of a bigger bill — they were invited to visit the president's luxurious villa just outside Moscow on their own. They were given tea, under the watchful eyes of a gaggle of TV cameramen and journalists whose vocabularies did not, on this showing, include the word 'unobtrusive.' Medvedev was dressed casually in jeans and a light jacket. Members of the band sported 'sunglasses and long hair.'[171]

Gillan took on the role of spokesperson, joking that he had always thought that politicians were supposed to be old men (Medvedev was 45 at the time). Ever technically minded, Morse busied himself with the retro-looking reel-to-reel tape deck that occupied the top of a nearby cupboard like a relic from the Cold War. The press pack having left, Medvedev's 15-year-old son, Ilya, jammed with the band on the guitar, Morse no doubt taking the lead role. Autographs were exchanged: these were to become highly significant over a decade later.

Airey — as unreliable narrator — remembered the meeting in a slightly garbled form: 'We met Dmitry Medvedev once. We drove through Moscow at a hundred miles an hour, down the wrong side of the road. The American Foreign Secretary, Robert Gates, had just had a meeting, so we were following in his path. Medvedev used to be an amateur DJ when he was 15 and he played Deep Purple records. He'd send a list of stuff he was going to play to the Communist Party and then completely ignore it.'[172]

Upon leaving, Ian Paice presented the President with a pair of drumsticks. Presumably, he had some spares for the gig that the band played in Moscow that night, the setlist including a hefty chunk of material from albums on which Morse had played.

Morse would no doubt look back on his Kremlin meetings as among the stranger incidents from his long career, but they served to cover an increasingly uncomfortable truth: that it was now nearly six years since *Rapture Of The Deep* had been unleashed onto an indifferent world and the creative well, for Deep Purple at least, had run dry.

The news from Morse's solo projects was not much more encouraging. *Angelfire* had been a pleasant diversion but was only the most minor of milestones. The Steve Morse Band was in the act of slowly fizzling out. *Out Standing In Their Field* is their last studio release as of this writing.

Speaking some time later, Morse clarified the situation: 'I have a great amount of respect for the guys in the band. I really wanted to write to their strengths and that was the main focus in putting those albums together. I think we had a really good touring trio with both versions of the band. They're wonderful people, so talented and easy to deal with. But life is moving along. Looking back, I do think, "My God, what a lucky find being able to play with Jerry Peek, Rod Morgenstein, Dave LaRue and Van Romaine."'[173]

Deep Purple had tried to keep fans returning to their gigs with various ruses, such as playing the *Machine Head* album in its entirety from start to finish (an idea that was abandoned after a couple of so-

so gigs), or by introducing a greater quantity of rarities into their set lists (which may also have been about preserving Gillan's voice since it shifted the emphasis very much towards instrumentation).

They were about to try something even more ambitious. As for Morse, he clearly needed a new project that he could really sink his teeth into. Fortunately, one — unrelated to Deep Purple — was just on the horizon...

13.
The Great Spectacular

As early as 2009, Morse had rather apologetically told the UK's *Birmingham Post*, 'Deep Purple are always trying to get started [on making a new album] but these tours keep popping up. Recording is very nearly a volunteer endeavour and touring pays most of the bills.'[174]

With no recent release to drive the touring, the need for novelty was now pressing. The band were slated to visit the US where they were all but unknown. How to draw out the punters? One idea suggested itself, as conductor Stephen Bentley-Klein explained: 'Purple were going to America to do a tour and they hadn't been there for a few years and they wanted them to come back with something different and they suggested an orchestra thing.'[175]

Morse described how it would work: 'This one isn't going to be orchestra-based so much as it's the rock band Deep Purple playing with strings and horns added for some colour texture.'[176] He was also bluntly candid about the reasons for doing it: 'One of the things we're trying to do is give people a reason to come out and play some nicer places. It also gives us an in, to nicer halls that wouldn't allow a, quote, "rock and roll show." If you have a bunch of people carrying violin cases, I guess it opens the door, you know?'[177]

This was not, then, to be a repeat of the orchestra tour from a decade earlier: the 'Concerto' was not going to be featured and the only special guests would be Bentley-Klein and whichever orchestra was being used (the plan was to source orchestras from the towns and cities in which the band played). It would not be 'classical Deep Purple' so much as 'expanded Deep Purple.' For Morse, it was another chance to break out of the straitjacket of heavy rock and indulge his love of crossovers.

Bentley-Klein, who was involved courtesy of his erstwhile

colleague Airey, set about scoring the orchestra, using tapes of current live versions of the chosen songs for reference. The task was challenging because rehearsal time for band and orchestra together was at a premium, largely because there wasn't any at all to speak of.

As Bentley-Klein reported, the original plan was for everyone to meet up for two to three days prior to the first show in Toronto. This was cut back to one or two and then to zero, barring a quick run-through in the afternoon of the first concert. Obviously, for such an ambitious endeavour, this was less than desirable. A chink of light was that, as the tour progressed, the music-loving Airey offered to attend orchestra rehearsals to provide some of the rock sound against which the non-rock musicians could play.

Bentley-Klein remembers how this came about: 'I had a two, two and a half hour, at most, rehearsal time and you'd have to stop and start all the time. I'm a great friend with Don and he just loves being involved with music and around musicians, so he would say, "If we're in the same town in the afternoon... whenever I can, I will actually come down to you and just play the parts with you."'[178]

He was soon joined by Paice, who found the process so enjoyable that he willingly turned up to lay down a rhythm track. With rehearsals now including band members, moments could be worked out — among the best in the final shows — in which the orchestra and keyboards combined during Airey's solo slot.

Despite the constraints, the concerts proved to be consummately enjoyable affairs. Where the orchestra was essentially just playing along to the band, they added little, but on those songs where strings and brass brought new dimensions, the effect was often startling. Entries in the Deep Purple repertoire such as, 'When A Blindman Cries', 'Hard Lovin' Man' and, pre-eminently, 'Perfect Strangers,' were transformed into whole new creations.

The tour wended its way from Toronto into the US, before transferring to Europe, where much of the pressure was removed by only one orchestra being used throughout, the New Frankfurt Philharmonia. The Montreux Jazz Festival 2011 was one of the stops for a concert that was filmed and recorded. Reviewing the resultant release, Wayne Perry of the *Associated Press* was, on the whole, positive, apart from castigating Gillan for replacing his trademark screams with, 'a flaccid falsetto that kills the whole buzz.' Of Morse's contributions, he remarked: 'Guitarist Steve Morse (previously of

Kansas and the Dixie Dregs) brings his own touches and flourishes to songs [Ritchie] Blackmore made famous and deserves kudos for bringing something new to the party.'[179]

The band and Bentley-Klein broke off from the tour in July to appear at the latest iteration of the Sunflower Jam, which was held at the Royal Albert Hall. This was a charitable enterprise, originated by Ian Paice's wife, Jacky, which aimed to raise money to provide complementary therapists and spiritual healers for cancer patients in British hospitals. The format was that various rock and pop stars would perform for free, the proceeds from ticket sales going to the charity. Previous concerts had been private affairs in small venues with invited audiences.

A particularly supportive participant had always been Jon Lord and so when the decision was taken for there to be a 'Superjam' in 2011, to which the general public would be admitted, he was very much up for it. He did not perform with Deep Purple, preferring instead to partner with his old friend Rick Wakeman (Bentley-Klein adding a touch of violin). Afterwards, Lord and his 'biggest fan' Morse chatted and made a few noises about working together. Neither could yet have known how fateful that conversation was to prove.

But future projects were destined to remain, for now, on the back burner because the indefatigable Morse already had his hands full. The producer Bill Evans had been developing a vision of a supergroup that would create a sound combining complex and virtuosic music with catchy and accessible songwriting; the soundbite was that he aimed to make new-fashioned music the old-fashioned way, whatever that meant. To this end, he approached Morse and his fellow Kansas alumnus Kerry Livgren as well as another, unrelated, Morse, Neal, with a proposition.

Neal Morse was a born-again Christian and erstwhile member of Spock's Beard. He was also a highly respected solo artist and had been a part — along with Dream Theater's drummer Mike Portnoy and others — of another supergroup called Transatlantic. He described how the idea for the new band got going: 'It was Bill who pitched me the idea of making a record with Steve Morse which, of course, I was very ready to jump onto. Opportunities like those don't come along every day.'[180]

Steve Morse added more detail: '[Evans] wanted to put me

together with Kerry again in some sort of writing project with Neal Morse. Neal and I came up with some song ideas, but when Kerry had his stroke, he couldn't travel and it ruled him out.'[181]

Livgren's stroke was quite serious, affecting not only his ability to make music, but to express himself at all. He required two surgeries to add stents to his carotid artery and was forced to relearn many rudimentary actions. In the long run, he made a partial recovery, but, as Steve Morse pointed out, it happened far too late for him to be involved in the incipient supergroup project. Evans suggested enlisting Portnoy as a replacement. Dave LaRue (who else?) came in on bass. Portnoy's pick was Pete Trewavas from Transatlantic, but Steve Morse worried that this would turn the whole venture into a recreation of that band with only the guitarist having changed. So, he approached his old sparring partner, the better to create something fresh and exciting.

An excellent instrumental quartet, the band still needed a singer and top line melody writer if it were to be what Evans wanted it to be. Over a hundred candidates were considered, none having the required x-factor. In the end, Portnoy suggested his friend, Casey McPherson, the almost unknown singer of the almost unknown Alpha Rev. McPherson impressed enough to get the gig, but comfortably the least among equals, he was all too aware of his position: 'I was elated but hoped that they wouldn't give me the boot on my first day.'[182]

His fears were quickly allayed because, 'I found it pleasurable to be the singer and just one of the writers, and Steve Morse was especially encouraging to me.'[183] This should surprise no one given that Morse's entire *Angelfire* project had been, at bottom, about giving an industry leg-up to a young hopeful.

Now a full band and monikered Flying Colors (American spelling), nine days of writing sessions were organised at Neal Morse's home studio for January 2011. The two Morses had already met to gauge whether there was any chemistry and had thrashed out the bones of two songs that would eventually end up on record, 'Blue Ocean,' and the epic, 'Infinite Fire.'

Neal Morse said of this: 'Steve and I had been trying to get together to collaborate — this was in 2008, or something like that — and Evans had talked to both of us about collaborating and when we got together we found out that it was a bit like a blind date, where he tells one person, "He really wants to date you" and tells the other person that "That person really wants to date you." He told me that Steve really wants to write with you and I said that I would really love to write with him.'[184]

An indication of the project's modus operandi came with Steve Morse vetoing a song that Neal Morse had already completed on the grounds that bringing anything too polished to the party would give the rest of the band no space in which to add anything. This was a particular danger because: 'Neal will often bring in a song idea, like, "Here's a song I wrote in ten minutes, while I was thinking about the other song I wrote this morning which is similar in key to the one that I wrote while I was eating breakfast" — he writes a lot of songs is what I'm trying to say.'[185]

Evans, having brokered the talent, handed production duties on the eponymously titled debut album to Peter Collins. This was Steve Morse's brainwave: 'I'm a big Rush fan, so I pushed pretty hard to have Peter Collins in there with us. He was very good at chiming in when we were in danger of losing the plot.' [186]

Neal Morse later humorously stated that Steve's real reason for bringing in Collins was to give the band someone to blame other than each other if the album did not turn out as they hoped it would. The bulk of the material came from that first session, with Collins playing the role of editor and arbitrator between competing ideas. Steve Morse: 'We go with the primitive vote method when we reach an impasse. If somebody hates it, we don't do it. If someone likes their way better than another, then we vote.'[187] After everyone else had left, Portnoy stuck around to record drum parts. Overdubs and re-recordings were added over the next six months as and when the band's members could find the time.

In other news, Deep Purple's orchestra tour had reached its conclusion, but that did not mean that Morse was done with orchestras. In August, coinciding with a break in the band's schedule, and mere weeks after the Sunflower Jam, Lord suddenly announced that he was battling cancer. His press release feigned an upbeat tone, stating only that the diagnosis would result in a scaling down of his touring commitments (he had spent the decade since leaving Deep Purple as a jobbing composer, working with orchestras to bring his works to audiences worldwide) and that he would continue to write music. Paul Mann described the mood of Lord and those closest to him, 'When the diagnosis happened, he will have known — like everyone knows — that pancreatic cancer is one of the most complicated cancers to treat and he would have known the situation he was in, but we always around him tried to stay positive.'[188]

It is perhaps serendipitous that Lord was, at that moment, preoccupied with the 'Concerto for Group and Orchestra.' Amazingly, while his — and Deep Purple's — activities over the previous few years had led to there being numerous live recordings of the piece now in existence, no studio version had ever been made. Putting that right was one way to keep active as Lord faced up to his illness. He and Mann had booked the Liverpool Philharmonic (which had performed the piece the previous year) for a number of sessions with the rhythm section. They were recorded in Liverpool. The tapes were then taken to Abbey Road Studios in London for the 'group' parts to be retrofitted.

Since Lord wanted this to be the definitive version of the piece, he decided that, rather than use a generic, and, frankly, anonymous, collection of session musicians, each part should be taken by someone with the style and personality to really bring out its particular qualities.

He also wanted to stress that it was his composition and not primarily a Deep Purple piece, so he initially balked at involving any members of the band. Lord himself played the keyboard solos, the vocals were split between Steve Balsamo and Kasia Laska for the first, lyrical, verses and the force of nature that is Bruce Dickinson for the later blues section.

What, though, about the guitar solos? Blackmore was not an option for all sorts of reasons and Morse was hampered by still being a member of Deep Purple. Frequent Lord collaborator Darin Vasilev and the blues powerhouse Joe Bonamassa ended up being chosen for the first two movements but finding someone for the third proved tricker. Lord and Mann agreed that what they really wanted was someone who could recreate Morse's magnificent performance at the Royal Albert Hall in 1999. Who could do that? A number of names were mooted. In the end, Morse was asked, his wider reputation presumably trumping his membership of the band that was being deliberately distanced from the project.

Morse described how he thought that this came about: 'This was Jon's first chance to do his own recording without being associated with Deep Purple, and from what I understand he didn't really intend to ask me to do it. He just got used to the way that I played some of the sections. He was describing to the guitarist maybe in too much detail, trying to get them to recreate the way that I did it. I guess it just got easier to ask me.'[189]

Jon Lord died on 16th July 2012. He never got to see the release of the studio version of the 'Concerto,' although Mann reassured fans that he did hear the final mix, which was completed just days before his death. For Morse, it was the bitterest of blows. He had worked with some wonderful musicians over the course of an increasingly long career and some had already gone, but Lord held a particular place of respect in his heart.

In the immediate aftermath, he described himself as 'in shock' and repeated his praise of Lord's capacity to run with musical ideas and help to make a song out of nothing. More touching were the personal details that he revealed which showed both men as human beings, rather than rock stars: 'We all love people that will pay attention to our kids, and years ago he charmed my (then) 5-year-old son Kevin with a Donald Duck imitation even while he was being hurried to get out of the dressing room and go to the green room for after show greetings.'[190]

Morse added that, as Lord went through the debilitating rounds of cancer treatment: 'I kept hearing hopeful, positive reports that they might be making progress, but his sudden death caught me totally unaware. I thought we would meet and do a recording project in the future when he recovered from the chemotherapy. Well, we sort of did, but I had to record it and send it to him, as we were in different countries.'[191]

Morse received other reminders of mortality at around this time. He contributed to a double album called *Tommy Bolin and Friends: Great Gypsy Soul* that was released in March 2012 as a tribute to the late, great guitarist. Consisting of Bolin's performances with new parts recorded and overlaid by his 'friends' (most of whom had probably never met him), it was, in many ways, not unlike *Gillan's Inn* or School of the Arts — at least as far as those involved — including Morse — were concerned.

He played on the track 'Crazed Fandango,' adding some licks that moved between the smooth and the manic. A minor entry in Morse's discography, it merits mention not only for the fact that Bolin was the only other person to have permanently replaced Blackmore in Deep Purple (on the outstanding 1975 album, *Come Taste The Band*), but for what that says about Deep Purple's self-image as a band.

Like Morse, Bolin had never been a heavy rock guitarist. His solo work was funky and bluesy with an emphasis on instrumentals. As a collaborator with others, he was very much tied to fusion; indeed, he had worked in the 1970s with Billy Cobham, who had been a member of that intersection point of all influences, the Mahavishnu Orchestra. Obviously, Deep Purple's members had always valued ability over strict stylistic compatibility.

The Flying Colors album also appeared in March, the mix having been completed at Electric Lady Studios in New York. As a piece of work, it reflects the diverse backgrounds of its creators, no single style emerging as the 'signature' one.

Morse reinforced this, saying that a single style was eschewed so that: 'Each song can live its own life.'[192] The likes of 'Shoulda Coulda Woulda' and 'All Falls Down' are driven by blisteringly heavy riffs and drumbeats. Elsewhere — 'Blue Ocean,' say, or 'Infinite Fire' — bouncy bass lines, not unlike those from the Dixie Dregs or Steve Morse Band, are the rule.

Morse's folky acoustic playing crops up here and there. It is, as might be expected, a pleasant listen and Evans' chief goal is certainly met — it is sophisticated music with a pop edge. But it is another rather overly slick product. Disconcertingly, it reminds the listener of nothing so much as Morse's Kansas albums from over twenty years earlier. The band must have agreed with this assessment as, in 2017, they put out *True Colors*, a version that was closer to the less highly polished raw recordings from the original sessions.

If Flying Colors was a major side project for Morse, it was not the only one that occupied him in 2012. He also headed off on tour to South America with Joe Satriani and another Dream Theater member, John Petrucci. The occasion was Satriani's G3 project, which was an annual event in which he gathered three guitarists (hence the name) for a series of concerts in which they showcased their music and jammed together.

He had a very singular vision for this: 'G3 is the best kind of competition, where nobody holds back and each guy brings his best. It heightens the experience on stage, and the fans pick up on it. We push each other, and you can only do that with friends, you can't do it with adversaries.'[193]

The line-up that year was stellar — that goes without saying — but said something about Morse that was becoming increasingly obvious… It can be illustrated by quoting his summation of Petrucci's abilities: 'John is amazing, he is taking the virtuoso thing to another level, he is really impressive. There is nobody that can do what he does. He always sounds great and he keeps getting better, it's scary… I think he is an alien from another planet.'[194]

Dream Theater, like Flying Colors, were firmly rooted in prog. Whether that was now Morse's signature style, or just another of the many to which he turned his hand, was a question that could only be answered by the next album on which he would appear — whatever that would be.

Morse's set for the G3 tour consisted of Steve Morse Band songs, such as 'Name Dropping' and 'Stressfest.' He then joined Satriani and Petrucci for a jam, ending with a cover of Neil Young's 'Rockin' In The Free World.' Morse and Satriani both being present, an opportunity existed for them to play something by the one band that they had it common; that, though, does not seem to have been the point of the exercise.

Flying Colors gigs in September — presumably when everyone could be got together — included a few of their original songs, the rest of the running time being bulked out with Dream Theater, Spocks Beard and Dixie Dregs covers. As a tour, it was quite wide ranging, taking in Europe as well as the US. The main benefit for Steve was that it finally promised a creative outlet beyond Deep Purple that had some longevity.

But speaking of Deep Purple, fans had begun to get used to the idea that the underwhelming *Rapture Of The Deep* was effectively it for new material. They were to be proven wrong, the catalyst being the reintroduction of someone from Morse's past who was about to become a big part of his present and future.

14.
Uncommon Man

Since his brief stint as producer for Kansas, Bob Ezrin had kept himself busy, making music, investing in tech, even putting out a charity single. Out of the blue, he was contacted by his friend Neil Warnock, who happened to be Deep Purple's booking agent, with the suggestion that he produce the band's next album. Of course, this made the increasingly large assumption that there would be a next album, but, willing to explore the possibility, he went to see the band play at Massey Hall in Toronto.

His immediate response was to be blown away by their virtuosity. In summing up his feelings, he foregrounded what has always been Deep Purple's main strength: 'They do this jam which lasts about ten or fifteen minutes where Morse steps up and is a total guitar god, and then Don backs him up with symphonic keyboards.'[195] His interest was piqued, but what he most wanted to do was recreate that live sound on record: 'It was not only essential to capture that sound, but it was essential that they heard it when they came into the control room for the playback.'[196]

Given their history — and the respect that Morse had for him — it might be expected that the guitarist would be his biggest advocate, but that is not exactly how it went: 'I was in favour of working with him,' Morse has said, 'and the other guys hadn't worked with him. And I was afraid if I had suggested to work with him, then the band wouldn't want to. So, I kept my mouth shut and waited for a common period and said, "Yes, I think he's great." Instead of pushing him.'[197]

A meeting with Ezrin was arranged at which he put the question directly to the band: what did they want to be? The answer they gave was Deep Purple, as in the band as it truly was, not as some radio-friendly, pre-packaged, approximation of Deep Purple. Not, perhaps, the kind of compromised product that Kansas became on the two albums featuring Morse.

The conversation requires some contextualising because 'being Deep Purple' did not mean the same as it would have done in the band's 1970s heyday. Then, it would have fairly and squarely referenced heavy rock. Yes, there would have been plenty of other influences, but their masterpieces, *In Rock* and *Machine Head*, are generically of a piece and very loud. By 2012, Morse, Airey and the advancing ages of the others had led to the mixing in of different textures. *Abandon* may have been in the old spirit of things, but everything since had begun a subtle shift towards the kind of prog that can be heard on *Flying Colors* and its ilk.

While working on the new material, Morse credited Ezrin with deconstructing his playing and changing it to more closely fit his overall vision for Deep Purple: 'He wants me to play more like [Pink Floyd guitarist] David Gilmour and less like I would. In other words, he wants something spectacularly melodic and simple. That's a huge challenge. What ends up happening is I do what I do and to some extent, I do bend to his wishes. He'll take out a couple or even several solos. He'll cut out pieces he thinks sound closer to what he's envisioning. So lately, I end up with solos that are more clean and simple.'[198] Morse had come a long way from the days when he wrote and produced everything himself.

Songs, though, were still generated in the old way — with considerable input from Ezrin — prior to any recording sessions taking place. Creativity was not a problem, Morse reporting that: 'We did three writing sessions over the course of a year and ended up with over twenty songs. I remember saying to the guys, 'Can we please stop putting new ones on the pile? I can't remember them all!''[199]

A theme of many of those songs was time, which proved to be central to the resulting album as a whole. Recorded in Nashville and titled *NOW What?!*, it includes several tracks that deal with the temporary nature of existence. Two — 'Uncommon Man' and 'Above and Beyond' — are explicitly tributes to Jon Lord. Others touch upon mortality in more oblique ways. The first single 'All The Time In The World' belies its hopeful title in its lyrics consisting of the words of someone who has wasted his life, the second, 'Vincent Price' takes a humorous approach by talking about the undead.

Morse articulated how he felt about this whole issue: 'Time has gone by very quickly and some cliches are cliches because they are true. And one of those cliches is that time seems to accelerate the older you get.'[200]

It is natural that such matters were on the band's mind as they worked. The dramatis personae of this narrative — their colleagues and friends — was ineluctably reducing in size. Most members of the band were not at their healthiest either, the constant touring taking its toll. This did not exclude Morse.

As early as 1997, Gillan had joked about how Morse had fallen off his bike, broken three ribs and still flown home during a break in the schedule to record an album. But that was as nothing compared to the problems that were beginning to afflict his hands, the parts of his body upon which his art most depended. He had worn a support glove before, but it was to become ever-more present in future years. Things were still manageable in 2013, but it would not be long before playing was a source of pain, necessitating a switch in technique.

Illness lay behind Morse's participation in the Jason Becker Benefit Concert in January 2013. Becker, like Morse, was a guitarist and, like Morse, legendary within the musician community. A one-time member of the 1980s speed metal duo Cacophony, he had more recently backed Dave Lee Roth in his solo endeavours. Tragically, he was arguably more famous for suffering from amyotrophic lateral sclerosis, otherwise known as Lou Gehrig's Disease. A degenerative and ultimately fatal motor neurone condition, ALS deprives its sufferers of all muscle control, affecting speech, cognitive function and, eventually, the ability to breathe. For any type of musician, it is particularly devastating.

The benefit concert, billed as 'Not Dead Yet,' took place at Slim's in San Francisco. The contributors were mainly guitarists, Morse being joined by, among others, Uli Jon Roth, Richie Kotzen and Gretchen Menn, a rare woman in the world of heavy rock and one who was originally inspired to take up music by hearing 'Tumeni Notes' from the *High Tension Wires* album.

The aim was to raise funds for Becker's ongoing treatment. While Morse's problems were not of the same order as Becker's, both were reminders that guitar playing is a physical activity that can be taken away on the whim of fate or happenstance.

On a happier note, *NOW What?!* was released in April. Thanks to canny marketing by its label earMUSIC, it arrived on a wave of anticipation and was a palpable hit. It reached the UK top twenty (the first Deep Purple album to do so in decades) as well as climbing to a very respectable position in the Billboard 200 in the US.

Reviews were mostly positive, with some reservations. AllMusic said of the album: 'Some things really shouldn't change and Deep Purple recognise that. They haven't changed a bit and the group's many fans are going to find this release comforting in that regard.'[201] This is actually a somewhat tin-eared interpretation; there can be little doubt that Deep Purple, with Ezrin as their conductor, had changed.

The same can be said of the market and the critical environment. For all its high placings, *NOW What?!* did not sell all that many copies. It did better than either *Bananas* or *Rapture Of The Deep*, but that is not saying much. The truth is that the efforts of record companies to keep the album as an art form alive had largely failed. Morse was right: recording was no longer a financially worthwhile activity. As for the album's reception, it is worth noting how far the consensus had shifted since *Abandon* — which had been panned.

Deep Purple, as a band and as an institution, were noticeably entering that old rocker territory marked 'uncriticisable.' In other words, it was now generally recognised that their fans were going to buy what they were selling regardless of its quality and the likelihood of the fan base growing or contracting was so low that it was frankly pointless to be too negative about it all. They were what they were.

An expanded edition of *NOW What?!* that included instrumental versions of some of the tracks (inessential), the B-side 'First Sign Of Madness' (desirable, not essential) and live versions of some of the album's songs (inconsequential) followed some months after the first release. It more-or-less coincided with the latest offering from Flying Colors, *Live In Europe*, which, as its name implied, had been recorded in Tilburg, Netherlands, in September 2012.

This faithfully reproduced the band's set, Morse justifying the track list thus: 'We didn't have much choice because that is the only material the band had plus we had to add some covers and identity pieces.'[202]

An overlap between Morse's projects was the inclusion of a raucous rendition of Deep Purple's 'Space Truckin'' as a hidden track on the third disc. *Classic Rock Revisited's* review sums up the attitude of the critics: 'This is the cream of the crop when it comes to flat out talent and ability… from performing to songwriting to instrumental mastery, it does not get any better than this in a live setting.'[203]

Or perhaps it could. Paul Mann has spoken of how conversations at the time of Jon Lord's funeral brought up the idea of somehow memorialising the great musician and composer. His music already did that, of course, but something bespoke was desired and what could be better than a live public event? From somewhere came the decision to make this the focus of the next Sunflower Jam and to hold it in Lord's (almost) spiritual home, the Royal Albert Hall. Paice gave the rationale: 'We wanted everybody on stage to be connected with Jon, either musically or personally. We needed to have that sort of camaraderie on stage.'[204]

In accomplishing this, the programme needed to encompass Lord's rock and classical sides. How to structure it posed some problems. Mann, who was the natural choice to conduct the orchestra, suggested a first half of classical music, followed, after an interval, by a rock concert. An alternative would have been a chronological arrangement mingling rock and classical pieces throughout the evening, but this was rejected as technically difficult and possibly anti-climactic.

An hour long set by Deep Purple would bring the evening to a conclusion, but, before that, a varied selection of Lord's classical pieces would be given an airing. A glaring omission was the 'Concerto for Group and Orchestra,' which, as Mann underlined, was left out because it could not be fairly represented with just a short extract and, anyway, it was well known — unlike much of the rest of Lord's oeuvre, which richly deserved its place in the sun.

It was all a fitting prelude to the later parade of rock royalty that graced the stage as an appetiser for the Deep Purple set. Rick Wakeman, Glenn Hughes, Bruce Dickinson, even Paul Weller, were slated to appear. Mickey Moody, Bernie Marsden and Neil Murray — not obscure names by any means — were relegated to 'second tier' status. Flying Colors may have been good, but this was a real supergroup! Blackmore and that other prominent Purple alumnus, David Coverdale were conspicuous by their absence, albeit that their reasons for staying away were not identical.

When they finally came on — after a fluffed introduction by the normally slick Dickinson — Purple played several songs, combining classics with more recent works. Both Lord tributes from *NOW What?!*

were essayed. Morse duelled with Bentley-Klein's violin on 'Lazy' (a call back to doing the same with Allen Sloan and Jerry Goodman in past lives). Morse also did his call-and-response audience singalong with 'Black Night.' The undoubted highlight, however, was a lengthy rendition of 'Perfect Strangers,' exquisite orchestral backing adding layers and textures that raised it to a whole new level. Perhaps this could not strictly be called fusion, but it nonetheless connected two genres brilliantly.

Of the event as a whole, the Deep Purple fan magazine *Darker Than Blue* wrote: 'A moving musical evening of highs and... well, more highs really.'[205] The ultimate 'high' was the finale, a version of 'Hush' on which most of those present, including the orchestra, played. Arguably, the recording of it (like that of Hendrix interrupting a live televised 'Purple Haze' to do an impromptu tribute to Cream) will become a connoisseur's classic in the future, so much is it filled with fun, improvisation and love. Morse spars with Airey and Rick Wakeman, Wakeman and Airey spar with each other, Gillan forgets to sing some of the song's 'la las' into his mic... It has a free form party feel to it that is ideal for the occasion. It also plays to Morse's strengths as an improviser and team player.

It was a fitting end to an evening notable for many things, not least that during it, Morse was freed — perhaps uniquely — from the duty to play a song that was dropped for not being primarily a Jon Lord creation: 'Smoke On The Water.'

15.
Collateral Damage

For its sufferers, knowing that osteoarthritis affects one-in-seven adults in the US is probably scant consolation. A degenerative and debilitating disease of the joints, it causes cartilage to break down such that bones have nothing to cushion them and they grind together, severe pain and stiffness being the result. The symptoms worsen over a period of years leading, eventually, to the moving of affected parts of the body becoming difficult, if not impossible. For a musician, it is not just an agonising affliction but a threat to their livelihood and, on a grander scale, a killer of their art. It had slowly been attacking Morse's wrists for quite a while but was now beginning to make its presence felt in the worst way possible.

'I'm genetically predisposed to having osteoarthritis,' he has said, 'For the last fifty years, I've been playing with a technique in which I bend my wrist on two different axes, as I twist it, in order to keep the heel of my right hand against the strings so I can create an open space in which every string is muted, except the string I'm playing on. I use two fingers and a thumb and an arched hand position.'[206]

He went on, 'It really helped me play with exceptional clarity and muting. There are a lot of advantages with it. The only disadvantage is it wears out your wrist after fifty years. But I was doing 10,000 notes a day... most people should be fine! Now I've had to switch to one finger and the thumb because I have arthritis in my right wrist.'[207]

He could have practised less, but that was never an option. As he has said, he had a responsibility to his audience. If people had bought a ticket to a show, travelled a long distance to see it (a probability in the US), paid for a hotel room and bought the merch, then the least that they deserved was the best performance that the musicians could possibly give. And being perfect, or as close to perfect as could be reached, was not a given.

Neal Morse quoted a colleague as having opined that a musician needs to be reaching 200% excellence before a show because half is lost once it starts. Steve refined that slightly by stating that he would not perform a song in front of an audience until he had successfully run through it ten times; playing it ten times and making mistakes, if only on two or three occasions, did not guarantee that the version performed in a show would not also fail. On stage, nothing can be repaired. There can be no overdubs, no cut-and paste fixes. The song as performed is what the audience gets, for better or worse. So, Morse could not go out unprepared — never mind that he was a supremely able improviser.

As he entered older age — the clock was rapidly clicking around to his sixtieth birthday — the osteoarthritis became worse. Had he been in any other profession, it would have been a good excuse to call it a day, but music had never been just a job to him. He simply could not give it up. His changing technique went along with more judicious choices of equipment to mitigate the effects of the disease as much as possible. There was too much to do for any other solution to be contemplated!

One such thing was the recording of the next Flying Colors album. Barely had *NOW What?!* slid out of the charts before Morse was back in the studio with his 'other' band. It is important to remember that, for all that the years between 2005 and 2013 were a dead patch for Deep Purple, for Morse, numerous initiatives came and went.

Of the new Flying Colors album, Portnoy took the view that it would reflect more closely developed relationships between the band's members (perhaps one meaning of its eventual title, *Second Nature*): 'The first album was very much a blind date. This time, there was an existing chemistry.'[208]

A relationship that was not renewed was that with Peter Collins. As much as everyone agreed that he had been a crucial presence on the first album, a decision was taken this time to dispense with the services of a producer, the band taking on the burden themselves. The method of recording was also different, band members getting together for a couple of days here and there to lay down tracks when their other commitments permitted. Things had to be that way because Steve was clear that the songs should be generated by the whole group. He therefore encouraged his band mates to turn up to writing and recording sessions with ideas for songs, rather than polished tracks. How the prolific Neal Morse felt about this has not been preserved.

From a technical perspective, the compositional methodology was novel and, for such venerable musicians, cutting edge; 'Before we got together for the first writing session we all did conference calls in Skype and tried out different ideas,' explained Steve. 'Each person could play something live, you know, most people did it in the studios and so we could hear but we couldn't play it together. So, it was like, I would say: so what do you think about this Casey? "Okay but let's try a D minor there" and he would play it on his guitar and then Neal would say: I was thinking about something for the bridge... and we talked through ideas like that, and then we would put our ideas on the Internet in a dropbox.'[209]

The release that this all led to is related to its predecessor only by having been produced by the same people. Musically, it is a considerable advance on what went before. Poppy rock is gone, its place taken by a full-on prog assault. Only one song ('Lost Without You') clocks in at less than five minutes (just), all the others running for five, six, seven minutes or more. The opener, 'Open Up Your Eyes', and the, nearly, closer, 'Cosmic Symphony,' are both well over ten minutes in length. Morse said of the former: 'We knew from the beginning that that was going to be a long piece sort of in the prog tradition of an epic that doesn't have to be a three-minute single, so we've got all kinds of moods [in it].'[210]

As this indicates, frequent changes in style and tempo within and between songs gives the album an expansive, monumental quality. This is only enhanced by such tricks as overlaying a choir on 'Peaceful Harbor.' Morse's description of how he played the final section of 'Cosmic Symphony' gives some hint of the complexity of the music: '[I played] that pentatonic (scale) stuff with the fourths and fifths and sliding... it was a real dreamy progression. A very simple major progression and so I just thought and tried to get a clean sound that had lots of air so I put delay and a lot of reverb and a bit of chorusing using my TC (electronics) pedals — I have a tone print in the delay that has already modulation on it so that it helps to swim a little bit.'[211]

Would it be fair to call *Second Nature* undisciplined, or even indulgent? To some extent, maybe. Morse's justification for how it turned out was convincing enough: 'I think the band intentionally was just not thinking about pop songs or anything like that... just let the music breathe and be relaxed about it — Don't underestimate the audience; in other words, let's assume the audience can handle lots of subtlety, complexity and changes of tempo.'[212]

But it is to be wondered what a producer would have made of it. It cannot be denied that Bob Ezrin had made a huge difference to Deep Purple's sound — as would become more and more clear, 'Ezrin Purple' was by no means the same as 'Old Purple' — would Collins have similarly reined in the excesses of Flying Colors as they moved forward? Who can say?

Reviews were enthusiastic; The Day wrote of it, 'While *Second Nature* is a very polished and slick-sounding record, the songs are viciously catchy. The performances are, as you'd expect, over the moon tremendous, and there are even a few tunes where — they can't help it! — Flying Colors stretch out with some extended and complex song structures. I was sceptical over the whole concept, but this is a fun and great and extremely accomplished record.'[213] The band, then, were doing a lot right, but it is difficult to completely allay the suspicion that, at an early stage, they had already reached Peak Prog.

Live dates in the US and Europe dropped the covers and concentrated on Flying Colors' own material. Lengthy versions of 'Open Up Your Eyes' and 'Cosmic Symphony' were included. Listening to the Morse of Flying Colors, it is obvious that he is enjoying his work. Indeed, he has said that a musician loving what they do — and being seen to love what they do — is the best way to win over any doubters or haters. These groups were not generally numbered among Flying Colors fans, but the same was not the case with Deep Purple.

Regardless of his tenure with the band having now overtaken that of Blackmore (and then some), Morse was still struggling for acceptance with some members of the Deep Purple fan community. Matters were not helped by the frequent rumours — exaggerated by the Internet — that moves were afoot to bring back together older line-ups.

In the run up to Lord's death, for example, serious conversations were had about effecting a reunion of the Mark III version of the band, in which Lord, Blackmore and Paice had been joined by David Coverdale and Glenn Hughes. That the whole wacky scheme never got off the ground was mainly a function of Blackmore's lack of availability (together with the fact that nobody had bothered to mention it to the — probably not interested — Paice).

More persistent was what came to be referred to, inaccurately, as 'Jon Lord's Dream', which was for all surviving members of Deep Purple, past and present, to play a concert together. It need hardly be said that no such dream seriously existed, as Lord himself explained: 'I said that was my dream [in a radio interview]. It was then picked up and touted as my intent as something that I was going to try and put together, which was nothing of the sort.'[214] Irritated members of the band, such as Glover, found themselves constantly having to deny that anything was being done to realise this dream that never was.

Morse was not of the same mind. In spite of the treatment that he continued to receive, he was open to bringing Blackmore back in some way: 'Fans would love it. It would be nice, I think, to see closure with everybody involved and the bad feelings put aside. I think they'd all get a kick out of it if they could get past the psychological barriers. I am a fan of music. I'm a musician. I am not a politician... As far as I am concerned, all members, past and present and future, of Deep Purple are welcome.'[215]

Such a comment may appear to be almost impossibly self-effacing in a world as fuelled by ego as that of the music business, but it is entirely in character. Morse was a collaborator, who, as he said, made the quality of the music his first priority.

Further proof of this came with his involvement in a pair of albums by the pop classical violinist David Garrett, *Garrett vs Paganini* and *Caprice*. On the latter, Morse backs Garrett's beautiful rendition of a Scarlatti sonata with some tasteful and understated electric guitar arpeggios. Occupying broadly the same territory as The Three Tenors — or, for that matter, 'Concerto for Group and Orchestra' — these again demonstrate how music as a form was Morse's chief concern.

Garrett was more rock 'n' roll in his sensibilities than Pavarotti, it must be said, but the desire to break down musical barriers and look for commonalities among genres and styles was a concern for both men. Morse was a willing accomplice, Garrett's attitudes chiming with his own: 'You have to fall in love with music,' Garrett has said, 'and, through music, you have to conquer the instrument.'[216]

In an oblique way, this comments on Morse's preparedness to include those who might be classed as rivals in his own work — they were not rivals to him, just other musicians who could bring something fresh to the table. In any case, the question of whether Blackmore, or any other past member of Deep Purple, should be invited back was soon to be aired in a very public way.

A bizarre example of Morse's commitment to music qua music was his work on a track called 'Off My Trolley' by a band called — believe it or not — Purpendicular. As their name implies, they began as a Deep Purple tribute band. By some act of persuasion on the scale of a Jedi mind trick, they had convinced Ian Paice to be their drummer and he had appeared on their albums and accompanied them on tour.

Accomplished musicians in their own right, they branched out into writing their own material which they put out as the album *tHis is the tHing*. All four instrumentalists from the current Deep Purple line-up guested, presumably at the behest of Paice. For Morse, it meant that he had transitioned from merely being support act to himself to being in a tribute band to himself.

More-or-less concurrent with such antics was a Flying Colors tour and associated live release, *Second Flight: Live at the Z7*. It is tempting to suggest that the title references Morse's two great passions, but it is not clear that he came up with it. The location, the Z7 Konzertfabrik in Pratteln, Switzerland, was chosen by Mike Portnoy, who had history with it. The concert from 12th October 2014, was filmed and recorded but, coming not long into the tour, proved difficult to get right. Irrespective of Morse's philosophy regarding practising, the band's members were still learning the tunes, necessitating some flying — so to speak — by the seats of their pants.

The album would merit scant discussion were it not for the fact that it was used to experiment with several innovations in recording and filming. No less than twenty-four cameras were employed, some being go-pros attached to instruments. Not only did this enhance the visuals, but it gave scope for the DVD to include several novel listening options; as the band's website stated: 'You can choose where you listen from in the Z7. The Audio Menu shows you a map of the venue, and you can hang at the front of the stage, or right behind the soundboard... In each place, you'll get a completely different 5.1 surround mix.'[217]

Another mix was intended to be heard solely through headphones — anticipating that many listeners would be playing the album version on smartphones — the rather arch name given to the process being 'headphone surround' (because 'we're not contractually obligated to be creative until the next album.')[218]

Joking aside, this, together with the ultra-modern way in which *Second Nature* was written shows how the band, in defiance of its members' ages, was prepared to adopt, indeed embrace, technology if it could improve the quality of the final product.

But all such debates and experiments were about to be spectacularly overshadowed. The Rock and Roll Hall of Fame came calling. For those who do not know, the RARHOF is essentially a museum, located in Cleveland, Ohio, founded in 1983 by Ahmet Ertegun, Chairman of Capitol Records. It is also an arbiter of what passes for significant in the world of popular music. Every year, a small number of acts (of any relevant genre) are 'inducted' into the Hall in a lavish ceremony held somewhere in the United States. Effectively the pop world's Nobel Prize, to be an inductee is esteemed a major honour. The only stipulation for consideration is that any potential nominee must have released their first recorded material at least twenty-five years earlier.

Like most things in rock, the Hall is treated by fans and commentators alike with a mixture of reverence and cynicism. Phil Arvia of the *Chicago Tribune* is only one who has brought out the tension: 'The Rock and Roll Hall of Fame inductees exist to sell tickets to the Rock and Roll Hall of Fame and Museum in Cleveland', he wrote, before qualifying the cold realism of the statement with, 'Of course, this is just one truth. Another is that the rock hall was founded by people who made careers in the music business, people who no doubt wanted to see their life's work validated and, hopefully, perpetuated.'[219]

Why Morse was not in the Hall was a mystery — one which, as of this writing, is still unsolved. After all, few living musicians of any kind have had more distinguished careers. His propensity for spreading himself thinly around projects may have worked against him: which of the many Morses should be inducted?

But whatever the reason, he remains on the outside, since the call was not for him but for Deep Purple. It came, though, with a couple of unpleasant caveats that would catapult him into a maelstrom not of his making but which would, nonetheless, place him in a very difficult position.

16.
Shoulda Coulda Woulda

Deep Purple had been nominated for the Rock and Roll Hall of Fame on at least one previous occasion but had been rejected on the frankly silly grounds that they were a one hit wonder (the hit being, probably, 'Smoke On The Water'). This is clearly more a reflection of the parochialism of the awarding committee than the band's profile and history.

Deep Purple were no longer a force in the US, it is true, but that is only to acknowledge American exceptionalism in such matters. Elsewhere, the conversation around whether the band would ever get in was becoming increasingly intense. In 2013, Gillan had joined it, taking a disingenuous line: 'Maybe it will happen one day, but if not, my diary is full and I'm very happy. It hasn't affected our career but it does concern the fans — that's who I feel for.'[220]

Ah, the fans. They were the ones who really cared. Well, they got their wish in 2016 when presumably it finally became known in Cleveland that Deep Purple had been around for the better part of fifty years on and off, mainly on, and had produced quite a lot more than just one song. It was good news for Morse, who was at long last going to be inducted into the Hall, if only as part of a band. Or perhaps not.

The citation only mentioned the first three line-ups — 'marks' — and not every member of those. For reasons that will forever remain undisclosed, the band's first bass guitarist, Nick Simper, was not included. This must have been more than an oversight because, despite being pointed out, it was not corrected at the time and has not been since. He joined the band at its inception and appeared on its first three albums, but he has never been inducted. Needless to say, then, that the names of all who had been members after the cut-off point of 1974 were likewise not on the invitation — the late

Tommy Bolin, Joe Lynn Turner, Airey and, naturally, Morse.

This would not have been too much of a problem had it not damagingly intersected with the band's ever-fractious politics. Lord, of course, was being honoured posthumously, but what of the others? If the organisers had hoped for a Four Seasons-style cultural moment by bringing back Blackmore and — Holy Grail of Holy Grails — tempting the first, lost, lead singer, Rod Evans, to come out of hiding and stand on a stage for the first time since 1980, they were to be disappointed. And what of Morse and Airey? They were in the current incarnation of the band: if they did not turn up, who would play the mandatory three songs that accompanied any inductee's official admission to the Hall?

The question of Blackmore attending proved to be so controversial that it almost caused the whole thing to be called off. Gillan stated his view in no uncertain terms: 'It would be unconscionable to think about bringing Ritchie in.'[221] He then doubled down by declaring that he would be staying at home himself, since to go would call for him to hob-nob with former colleagues he would rather not see, while ignoring current colleagues he definitely would. For his part, Morse has said that he took the opportunity to state again that he would relish playing with Blackmore: 'The mediator part of me came out. I was, like, "I wish you guys could just do something and hug each other and deal with it for a day."'[222]

Ultimately, Blackmore conveniently resolved the problem by announcing that he would not be taking part in the ceremony. The 'official' reason given by the Hall itself was that he was due to have surgery and so was simply not available. Blackmore rather spoiled this attempt at face-saving by publicly stating that he had been prevented from going by the band's management (although how much power they would have had to enforce the ban is unclear).

David Coverdale supported this view sometime later, suggesting that the management had even tried to bar him and Glenn Hughes from making speeches. Years later, Gillan denied everything, claiming that Blackmore had been invited to perform 'Smoke On The Water' with his erstwhile colleagues but had refused.

The whole, rather tedious, business rumbled on for far longer than it should have done. Indeed, at the time of writing, it has yet to be fully resolved. But at the heart of it stood one man who was only there for the music and who selflessly agreed to perform at an event that many would have taken as their public humiliation — Steve Morse.

It is to his credit that ego is not his most notable characteristic; if there is any justice, he will be back on the Rock and Roll Hall of Fame stage in his own right at some point. And perhaps his most eloquent statement on the matter came in the title of a single on which he guested in 2016, 'Don't You Tell Me Not To Play Guitar' by Dorian Chiiwahwah Phallic.

On the night — a compromise having been reached to the effect that inductees would speak while the band, as it then was, would play — he graciously listened to the interminable speeches of those lucky enough to be inducted. Gillan went in to bat for him and Airey, talking about how the two had been parts of the living, breathing band for years, but were — incomprehensibly — being left out.

Coverdale, for some reason, spent much of his allotted time harping on about his own band Whitesnake (which stands zero chance of ever getting into the Hall). From the rest it was all 'thank yous' and 'we couldn't have done it withouts…' (Blackmore's name only briefly appearing).

The formal nonsense over with, Morse and Airey made their contributions to a short set consisting of 'Highway Star,' 'Smoke On The Water' (of course) and 'Hush.' As if to underline what the Hall were missing, the opportunity for virtuosity was taken with alacrity, 'Smoke' ending with a crowd-pleasing jam and 'Hush' being preceded with a short run through of Booker T and the MGs' 'Green Onions.' In the end, the event was memorable — not always for the right reasons — but way short of satisfactory. Jon Lord's Dream had turned into the Fans' Worst Nightmare.

Even so, it could perhaps have been seen as a cap to the band's career since speculation about for how much longer they could continue was becoming a constant theme. Stephen Bentley-Klein was only one of many who noted that the band members' health was not at its best. In 2016, Paice suffered a mini stroke that, while recoverable, necessitated the cancellation of several gigs. Then there was Morse's osteoarthritis. The moment for a dignified retirement was upon them, with the Rock and Roll Hall of Fame induction as a glorious full stop.

What they, rather perversely, did instead was to make an album with the defiant title, *InFinite*. Whether it might actually be their last output was left somewhat ambiguous. In press releases, various members hedged their bets, saying yes, no, maybe. Morse's response was an enigmatic half-nod and mischievous smirk. Airey was the most definite, quipping that, as far as he had been concerned, the last album had been the last album.

Recorded in Nashville, *InFinite* was again helmed by Ezrin. As a collection, it is less introspective than *NOW What?!*, although how far it meets Ezrin's avowed intent to 'put the deep back into Purple' is questionable. From a lyrical perspective, most of the songs fall into one of two camps: banal political statements ('Time For Bedlam,' 'Hip Boots,' 'Birds Of Prey') or seedy short stories, allegedly based on real events ('One Night In Vegas,' 'Get Me Outta Here,' 'On Top Of The World').

Of the former, the impetus was given as Gillan's increasing disgruntlement with the world. He was, he said, an angry young man, then a complacent middle-aged man and now an 'absolutely fucking furious' old man. Best of the lot are the rather moving 'Johnny's Band' (try listening to that one without getting something in your eye) and 'The Surprising.'

The second of these comes closest to embodying Morse's impact on the album and, indeed, the whole ethos of Deep Purple. The title seems meaningless — the words 'the surprising' never appear in the opaque lyrics — until it is realised that it is a contraction of 'The Surprising Mr Morse', a provisional title occasioned by the song springing from an odd little riff that the guitarist happened to be playing during a writing jam.

The finished piece cannot be described as heavy, its changes of direction and tempo being far closer to prog. It does not sound much like a classic Deep Purple song — but it would fit perfectly on an album by Flying Colors, especially given that, at six minutes, it is longer than most of the tracks with which it is partnered (the exception being a cover of The Doors' 'Roadhouse Blues' that goes on for about a week).

Reviews of the album were respectful-to-good. The *Bristol Herald Courier*, for example, wrote of it: 'Morse and keyboardist Don Airey... deserve particular credit for keeping the trademark Purple sound fresh on tracks like "Time For Bedlam" and "All I Got Is You" with the intricate interplay between guitar and keyboard solos, saturated in the keyboard distortion that makes this band's sound so instantly recognisable.'[223]

Classic Rock called it, 'A feast of wanton organ and quasi-classical keyboard curlicues, bolstering bass from Roger Glover and percussive surges courtesy of Paice. Gillan, meanwhile, is in grand over-the-top form, trying a little too hard, perhaps, to keep up with the heavy metal kids, effing and blinding throughout.'[224]

The album was a hit in most of the markets in which it was released... sort of... It reached some high chart placings, including a few number ones and a top ten placing in the UK (even the normally indifferent Americans liked it enough to send it well up the Billboard 200 chart), but that is not to say that it actually sold all that many copies. It got nowhere close the number achieved by *Purpendicular*, for instance, and that had languished in the outer rims of most charts.

A tour in support of the album was given the 'cover all bases' title The Long Goodbye. The idea was to prepare fans for the possibility that this might be the end while allowing space for a change of mind if letting go proved just that bit too hard to do (spoiler: it was).

Gillan explained that the impetus had come from the illnesses that were now a fact of life: 'Everyone in the band was unwell; we all had health problems, which have been well documented and I think somebody — I can't remember who said it, probably somebody from the office — said, "Do you guys wanna call it a day?"'[225]

For Morse, the title was more definite: he planned this to be his goodbye: 'For me, personally, it's a farewell tour. As for the other guys, I think they will still be playing, perhaps in other groups, special projects or as guests. I also plan to stay in music, but not so actively as now. But you do realise that, when the music for so many years is the most important place in your life, [it's] impossible in one day to abandon it. In general, I know that the guys are not going to retire. They would rather die onstage than in bed.'[226]

The tour kicked off in Romania in May 2017. Of most note were the set lists, which showed more creativity than had been the case of late. Perennial opener 'Highway Star' was bumped to the encore, the equally raucous 'Time For Bedlam' taking its place. Several other new songs were also included, 'The Surprising' being most... surprising. Other rarities and Morse era songs filled out the runtime. This was not to last.

By the time the show rolled into North America, *InFinite* was already beginning to disappear, the band's early seventies heyday making its inevitable return. The tour was to rumble on for the better part of the next two years, taking in, as well as Europe and North America, South America, Mexico and Japan. A notable stop was at the BBC's Radio Theatre in London, where, in an echo of the 'In Concert' series from the early seventies (which produced one of their most treasured live albums), the band performed a truncated version of their set for broadcast.

This would have been enough to occupy most people, but Morse was far from 'most people.' On 3rd July 2017, Rod Morgenstein appeared on YouTube to make the following announcement: 'It is official! After forty years, the original line up of The Dixie Dregs are getting together to start touring in February of 2018 and we hope we see you out there on the road.'[227]

There was some uncertainty as to whether this was a formal announcement, Morse saying: 'I don't know if Rod jumped the gun a bit, if that was the official moment or not. We're asking a lot of the market to get people out. But anybody who's interested in music — whether it's instrumental music or just likes rock, or just likes weird stuff, or wants to hear people play instrumental stuff — this is sort of a once-in-a-lifetime deal.'[228]

The big news, of course, was that it was the 'original' line-up that was set to feature. It is to be wondered whether Morse saw an irony, given that the opportunity for something like Deep Purple's original line up to work together again — at the Hall of Fame induction — had not been taken. The motivation was said by Andy West to have come from him, Morgenstein and the band's manager Frank Solomon happening to notice that 2017 was the fortieth anniversary of *Free Fall*. There was also the fact that, of all the many people who had played regularly in the Dregs, the five who made the album were pretty much the only survivors.

Spurred on by this, they started to email each other and others about a possible reunion. Davidowski was the most difficult to find. West has talked about how he had been the only one to not stay in something like regular touch with his former colleagues and had no real Internet presence, so tracking him down was not easy. Intrigued enough to at least try something, Morse invited them all down to his place to jam and see how things felt (this happened in January 2017) and, as West said: 'It felt pretty darned good, so we said, "Why not?"

So, it turned into [the tour].'[229]

Giving the tour the title of 'Dawn of the Dregs' the band designed a set list that stressed *Free Fall* without focusing solely on it. All of the inclusions, as far as could be accommodated, were from the line-up that had made that album. While this was a natural direction, it was not taken lightly, especially by Morse: 'The tour was my biggest challenge. I wrote almost all of that music when I was in my twenties. Things were just so easy then, but there were still parts of the Dregs' set that were hard to play even when I was twenty. Now, imagine, with everything going on with me, trying to get ready for that.'[230]

For his band mates, though, he had nothing but praise: 'It's the comfortable history we have. Andy West and I had a connection going back to high school. We were working on music back then. There's also the shared humour of the band and not fitting in with the music business but trying to make a living anyway. Rod Morgenstein is also the nicest guy you'd ever want to meet, as well as being one of the most talented musicians.'[231]

Morse also mentioned Sloan's commitment to learning his parts and Davidowski's refusal to let anyone else carry his keyboard, despite being a sprightly seventy-five years old at the time. It is not difficult to spot a difference in tone between such utterances and the ambivalence, if not weariness, that characterised anything he said about Deep Purple.

An issue that Morse may not have expected was around the band's name. It had been changed before, but for different reasons than those now fuelling conversations. Over time, the word 'Dixie' had acquired unwanted associations with the Civil War Confederacy and everything for which it had fought, making it controversial. As statues of Confederacy figures were pulled down all over the South, the word was dropped from many places in which it had once been prominent.

Dolly Parton's attraction Dixie Stampede became the more vanilla Dolly Parton's Stampede and the country band Dixie Chicks rebranded themselves, underwhelmingly, The Chicks (either choosing to ignore, or not notice, that 'chicks' in this context is no more the stuff of bien pensant dinner party conversation than 'Dixie').

In the case of the (Dixie) Dregs, a considerable irony was that Morse, a 'Yankee' by birth, was the only member who actually lived in the South. His attitude was to dismiss the conversation as irrelevant: 'Things are going a bit too far. We have all sides covered. It's just a name. We used to play "Dixie" in a minor key with three-part harmonies. It was a spoof. People got the wrong idea', adding, 'We're the Dixie Dregs. That's who we've been since we formed.'[232]

Again, Morse was keeping his political cards close to his chest. He just did not want to get into arguments about ideology and, in the event, the band's name was the cause of little-to-no comment.

As for the tour, it lived up to its 'old guys get back together for fun' billing in being short and geographically limited. Getting going in North Carolina in March 2018 it wended its way across — mainly — the South, before ending on home turf in Atlanta at the end of April. Gigs at several House of Blues venues were a reminder of other past glories for Morse. The set list was, as promised, replete with older tunes, with the likes of 'Twiggs Approved', 'Odyssey', 'The Bash' and, naturally, 'Take It Off The Top' all being dusted off.

The shows were very well received. Alan Cox, writing for *Sonic Perspectives*, spoke for most: '[The tour] acts as a long overdue reunion among old friends who are having a wonderful time revisiting a collection of musical conversations that are being updated with whatever the members have to say in the here and now.'[233]

On whether the tour really was a dawn of the Dregs, a new start, West was cagey: 'It's cool to be doing it. And that's really as far as we're taking it. I'll give you an example. We got our old crew back together. And the sound man and I share a birthday. The same exact day and year. And we were both excited about the tour. Two weeks before the tour, he has a heart attack and dies. And that's the reality of things at this point in life.'[234]

As it happens, it was not to be the last Dregs reunion, but, for now, everyone had lives to get back to — in the case of West and Sloan, beyond showbiz. For Morse, commitments to his two biggest projects needed to be fulfilled. Further touring was also impacted by the small matter of a global pandemic...

17.
Clearly Quite Absurd

A highlight of *Purpendicular* is 'Somebody Stole My Guitar,' a shaggy dog story about a man getting so drunk on tequila that he forgets to guard his beloved instrument, which is taken 'from the back seat of [his] car.' Gillan has often claimed that most of his lyrics are based on true stories. In this case, he might well have been in earnest, but the song could also have been a foretelling of the future. On 7th March 2018, as Morse was loading his gear at Lincoln Theatre in Washington DC for a Dregs gig, somebody stole his guitar. It was a Buscarino electric/acoustic — very valuable and very precious to Morse.

In an effort to get it back, he appealed to fans and offered a 'no questions asked' reward. So desperate was he that he enlisted the help of veteran rocker Steve Vai, who shared the call through his own networks, stressing how much the instrument meant to Morse.

Fortunately, and in a twist worthy of a thriller, the tale ended well, or as well as could be expected. Joe Bonamassa, of all people, was contacted by two mysterious characters named only as Mark and Bryant who supplied him with a tip that resulted in the guitar being retrieved and sent back to Morse via the equally unlikely figure of the producer Bill Evans. By all accounts, the individual who took it was remorseful and grateful for Morse's clemency.

Beyond the Dregs reunion, the Long Goodbye tour dragged relentlessly on, resuming in May with a show in Moscow, a year after it had all begun. From there, much schlepping around Eastern Europe ensued until the charabanc finally reached the West with a show in Albi, France, in July. For Morse, who had been unequivocal in stating that it would be his last tour with Deep Purple, its — in more ways than one — infinite nature must have been increasingly bemusing. He had said that he wanted to be there when the band finally threw in the towel, but there seemed no prospect of that happening any time soon. Some towns and cities had been visited more than once during the tour — how many goodbyes did they need?

But a break was coming up in the form of a revival of Flying Colors. Having been in abeyance for the last few years, they performed a couple of warm up gigs at the tail end of 2018 and the beginning of 2019 before appearing at 'Morsefest' on August 30th.

This annual weekend event had been curated by Neal Morse since 2014 and took place at his local church. The bizarre name was a coinage of Portnoy — who presumably meant it as a joke — and not approved by Neal himself. It proved impossible to alter once it was out in the world. Still, it was, frankly, appropriate because, for the most part, the acts who appeared were those with which Neal Morse was involved.

For the 2019 iteration, the name was especially apposite, since Flying Colors, complete with Steve Morse, and The Neal Morse Band topped the bill. In retrospect, the former's appearance can be viewed as hors d'oeuvres for a new album, which was shortly to be released.

In some ways, calling the album 'new' is to ask a three-letter word to do a lot of heavy lifting, sessions for it having taken place as early as December 2016 at Steve's studio. No further work was done until the end of 2018, when Portnoy took a trip to Nashville to record some parts at Neal Morse's studio.

Speaking in December 2019, LaRue described how the album came together: 'The first writing session we had I guess was like five years ago, or something. We had some technical problems on the session, and we ended up not finishing enough material for a record. We got about 70% of it written, so we had to book another session and it took us three years to find a window when all five of us can get together. This past December, a year ago now, we finally found some time. We got together for a couple of days and we wrote the rest of the album.'[235]

The sessions produced *Third Degree*, which followed the tradition of titles that included a numerical pun. Released in October 2019, LaRue called it the band's best work and it is hard to argue with his judgement. The usual combination of heavy rock, highly commercial melody writing and musical complexity, it is sometimes a little too artsy for its own good — characteristically for the band — but, even so, features some catchy songs.

'The Loss Inside' alternates blistering riffs with quieter moments driven by funky bass; the Hammond organ brings a soupçon of Deep Purple to the recipe. 'Cadence' incorporates several changes of direction into its string-backed medieval folkiness.

'Last Train Home' — the first of the album's epics — starts as classic blues before settling into a soft rock vocal section driven by Steve Morse's intricate guitar picking.

'Geronimo' is unusual — funky, moody and restless of structure. Of it, Steve said: 'At some point in every album, I try to force Dave to give us a bass figure that we can build upon. Case came up with a great, quirky vocal melody and Neal and I worked on the weird, jazzy chords that I love so much before the chorus.'[236] And so it goes on... Everything is enjoyable, pleasant, effortlessly competent.

Reviews were, as ever, strong, with the occasional dissenting voice. Pete Pardo said of it, 'Musically, it's not that different from their first two albums. Flying Colors try very hard to just be an accessible melodic rock band with a lot of progressive rock flourishes and I think they do that very, very well on this album. The band is starting to gel.'[237]

The *Prog Report* described the album as, 'The result of great songwriting, brilliant musicianship, amazing harmonies and undeniable melodies.'[238]

This was all nice to hear and read, but chart wise, the album was nothing to get too excited about: number eleven in Switzerland was about as good as it got (which does beg the question of why the band's highly regarded personnel were unable to mobilise the fan bases from their other projects to get behind them on this...).

A short tour had already started with Morsefest, which debuted 'You Are Not Alone' and 'Crawl' (the album's other epic), but got going in earnest a couple of days after the album's release, the setlist switching to one largely composed of new material. Dates in Europe included one in London that was recorded and released as *Third Stage*, again continuing a tradition of quickly following up a studio album with a live companion (the Morsefest performance was also eventually released).

Whether Flying Colors had any future was about to become a moot question. The tour over, the space in which to consider next steps was not easily identifiable. Deep Purple, on the other hand, were more than ready to record their next album, the third with

Ezrin as pilot. This time, the recordings took place in London, at British Grove Studios in November 2019. Nashville was used only for the recording of some orchestral backing: yes, indeed, orchestral backing. The band, inspired, it can be posited, by the combination of Ezrin and Morse, had come a long way since *Bananas*, when bringing in additional performers had caused a near mutiny among fans.

The Long Goodbye tour finally petered out in December with a gig in Cluj, Romania. It was clearly not a goodbye, or even much of a 'see you later,' since fresh recorded material was about to hit the street and would need the oxygen of live dates to boost its sales. The latest album, *Whoosh!*, was slated to be released in June 2020. But it was to fall foul of that blackest of swans, the Covid-19 pandemic.

Originating in the Wuhan province of China, the novel coronavirus in question spread like an Internet meme around the world, affecting old and young alike, causing spikes in health-related deaths and generally creating panic wherever it was reported.

As the number of cases rose exponentially, governments everywhere scrambled to devise some response. The banning of public events — so-called 'super-spreaders' — happened early, thus nixing the tour plans of any and all music acts. Labs everywhere raced to develop a vaccine, a whole slew of conspiracy theories being an unexpected by-product of their efforts.

The most drastic measures were still to come. Two phrases entered common parlance: 'social distancing' and 'lockdown.' On the advice of the World Health Organisation, people were told not to get within a few metres of each other and to ensure that they were wearing surgical masks at all times. They were also compelled to remain at home — locked down — except in very exceptional circumstances. For those who were able, working from home became the new normal. For those who were not, there was nothing to be done other than to sit the pandemic out, hoping that not just they, but their jobs, would survive what felt like a dry run for the apocalypse.

In every country (apart from Sweden), streets were empty, town and city centres were deserted, parks were abandoned. On football pitches, no ball was kicked. On stages, no poor players strutted and fretted their hours. Shops were locked up. Front doors were closed and left closed. Initially, the hope was that it would all last a couple of weeks, after which, the virus would have slipped out of the population and everyone could get back to their lives. But a couple of weeks became a month. A month became two months. The situation was beginning to acquire a sickening air of permanence.

The release date for *Whoosh!* was coming up. On the basis that shops were not open and, anyway, getting copies to them would be difficult, it was pushed back to August. This rather forgets the fact that the music that the album contained would mainly be listened to via the pandemic-proof medium of download or streaming; but the publicity around the delay was welcome.

As for the members of the band, they went home and stayed there. A dress rehearsal for retirement? Glover was quick to shoot that idea down: 'As much as we all loved the opportunity to have all this additional time with our families, it's clear that none of us are ready for a life without music and artistic expression just yet.'[239]

Morse retreated to his farm and fixed what needed to be fixed and bundled hay and gave lots of interviews over the internet. He took with him a supply of anti-bacterial baby wipes procured from Mexico when the band were there for a gig — pretty much their last before the huge tour planned to promote the upcoming album was postponed.

He bought the wipes at the behest of his wife Janine who had noticed that such items were no longer available in shops. She could see what was coming and was already preparing for it. Morse's first fourteen days back home were spent in quarantine in a trailer rather than his house. This exigency was necessitated by his adult daughter, who still lived at home, having a condition that made her unusually susceptible to the damage that could be done by covid.

Sadly, this was not to be the only personal problem to hit Morse at this time. In September of 2021, his mother passed away. He was careful to stress that she had been covid negative and had been an early vaccine adopter. Blood clots that she suddenly developed in her lungs were to blame. It happened when the worst of the pandemic was over but restrictions had by no means been completely abandoned. That it was a tough time for Morse is evident from his social media posts on the subject.

More mundanely, Deep Purple's tour had yet to get going and nobody could say for sure when, or if, it would. The initial year-long postponement was extended again — by another twelve months. It was in danger of being in support of an album that had long since been forgotten. By the time it finally happened, though, a good deal had changed that could not have been predicted at the time of its planning.

Before that, (and to jump back in time a little) *Whoosh!* came out as per its revised schedule. It was the latest Deep Purple album to be technically a hit. As a piece of work, it is arguably the most satisfying of the Ezrin albums, which have been labelled by some fans — although never by the band — the 'Time Trilogy.'

It perfects the formula developed during the Ezrin era — and perhaps the whole Morse era. Songs like 'Throw My Bones' and 'We're All The Same In The Dark' have classic Deep Purple riffs while combining guitar and keyboard sounds as only Morse and Airey — not Blackmore and Lord — could.

'Nothing At All' brings in baroque notes and Airey gleefully quotes the work of other composers in his solos. The song, though, that most epitomises the band's developing sensibilities is 'Man Alive.' A minor masterpiece, it combines actual strings, a killer riff, changes of tempo and tone, dissonance and a fabulous guitar solo. If ever there was a song that could only have been produced by this 'mark' of the band, then this is it.

The 'last' track — apart from 'Dancing In My Sleep', which, for some reason, is labelled a 'bonus' — is a cover of 'And The Address,' which was the very first track from the very first Deep Purple album. An instrumental, the lead players do not try to copy the solos from the original, opting to make it their own. The message is bludgeoning in its obviousness: the party's over; do not expect any more albums; this is it; retirement.

Well... okay, but, first, the album had to be taken on the road and that showed no signs of being possible as the 2020s continued to make their spluttering start. Morse — in whichever of his many guises — could do nothing but wait for things to change. Some of the people from his various circles kept themselves amused by pursuing side interests. Neal Morse followed something of a trend by producing a series of entertaining YouTube videos in which he chatted to other musicians, Steve Morse among them. For Deep Purple, Bob Ezrin had a different idea, an interim project, something to bridge the gap and keep the momentum from recent releases going.

The only possibility was an album (so much for 'And The

Address') and since being in the same place at the same time was not an option, it could hardly consist of jam-generated new material. It was decided to record and release an all-covers album. For a creative band like Deep Purple, this seemed to be an unprecedented step into territory that would, at best, divide the fan base.

In reality, it was not as radical as it appeared. The 'Mark I' version of the band had produced two albums comprised partly of covers (although Gillan and Glover had not been involved with either), both *NOW What?!*, and *InFinite* had included cover versions and, in any case, cover albums had become something of a fashion in recent years, with everyone from Bryan Ferry, to Saxon, to Bob Dylan adding to the genre. Nonetheless, a Deep Purple covers album was a strange prospect.

Gillan was most sceptical (despite the band that he fronted during Deep Purple's 1976 to 1984 hiatus — named, with becoming modesty, Gillan — having enjoyed considerable success with cover versions), saying: 'I was totally against it to start with. I thought that Deep Purple purists, myself among them, would see something like this as criminal, metaphorically speaking.'[240] He followed up the metaphor when asked what he had done during the lockdowns by answering that he had been turning to crime, in doing so supplying the album's title.

It was about all that he contributed, because, when selecting the songs to be covered, his ideas were roundly rejected. He did not take offence, stoically accepting that, as primarily an instrumental band, the tracks needed to reflect what the instrumentalists wanted to play.

The main criterion for inclusion was the extent to which a song could be 'Purpleised,' which did not mean improved as such, just internalised, reinvented, personalised. This is where the whole project mainly fell down, the selections being uninspired at best. Fleetwood Mac's 'Oh Well,' Love's '7 And 7 Is,' Cream's 'White Room'... all great songs, but did they need to be 'Purpleised'?

'Shapes of Things' was Morse's second pass at what had become a standard and it ended up being the lesser of the two. Some choices were simply bizarre: Louis Jordan's 'Let The Good Times Roll', Huey Smith's 'Rockin' Pneumonia and the Boogie Woogie Flu...'

From Morse's perspective, the most incomprehensible was Johnny Horton's 'The Battle Of New Orleans.' He could not get his head around why a British band would want to sing a song that is not only about the British getting their asses kicked but celebrates the fact. He was given a rapid primer in the British sense of humour.

As a story, this is quite charming, but it does illustrate the cultural differences between himself and his band mates — differences that twenty-seven years as a member had done nothing to alter.

The album was recorded using some of the technology-enabled techniques that Morse had perfected with Flying Colors and that, in a more primitive state, had been behind *Gillan's Inn*. Glover explained how the process occurred: 'Once we'd chosen the songs, a few of us in the band did demos of them — me and Steve Morse and Don Airey. We sat down with a drum machine and a couple of keyboard or guitar parts, or whatever it may be, and did a very basic demo — which went into a pool in Nashville governed by Bob Ezrin and he farmed it out to all of the people that needed to put solos on or this that and the other. Since we've all got home studios — in this day and age your computer is a home studio — that's how we did it. And it took quite a while to do it.'[241]

Ezrin was described as the 'conductor' who brought everything together. Morse stated that he distributed the chosen songs among the band's members for the demos on the basis of what he thought would work for given individuals: 'In my case,' Morse said, 'The Yardbirds and, of course, Eric Clapton with Cream and an old rock and roll tune that I always loved called "Lucifer" by Bob Seger — something that I heard him play when I was a kid, heard him play live.'[242]

As for 'Purpleising', he justified his changing of songs with the wry comment, 'I think the composers of this song really meant to do this…'[243] He also explained how his continuing wrist problems influenced how he played certain sections, notably the arpeggios from the end of 'Oh Well': instead of turning his wrist — which was painful — he adopted a technique of picking from the elbow. In practical terms, this made little difference to what the listener heard, although it meant that Morse had to relearn picking across two strings, the better to give a fuller, more complex sound.

All of this working away in private studios behind the scenes meant that the band were able to keep the album a secret until very nearly its release date. The first intimation of it came from a website that appeared seemingly from nowhere called TurningToCrime.

com, the sole context of which was a series of 'mugshots' of the band's members and a countdown clock that would reach zero on 6th October.

No other information was given, which sent fan forums into meltdown speculating on what it might mean. It was not that long since *Whoosh!* had come out and so few expected a new album. One idea was that it would be an announcement — much prepared for — of final retirement (the mugshots perhaps implying that the band would be 'going away for a while'). When the news came out that it was indeed to be a new album, the rumour mill's second cycle centred on its nature: surely not a collection of covers?

The album was unusual in several respects — not merely that it consisted exclusively of other artists' material. It was also not all from a single genre — jazzy standards rubbed shoulders with skiffle which shared space with blues. The closest any got to being heavy rock was a brief run through of part of Led Zeppelin's 'Dazed And Confused' in the closing medley.

Most startling was just how many other musicians appeared on the album, backing the core band. Brass, backing vocals, fiddles, even a squeezebox all served to fatten the sound. It is difficult to imagine the band under Blackmore allowing its sound to be augmented — or diluted. It says much for how relaxed everybody now was and how much Morse — and, no doubt, Airey — had been able to broaden the band's sonic palette. None of which is to say that 'Jon Lord's Dream' had suddenly become a reality.

Reviews were generally positive, most focusing on the notion that the album was conceived of as 'fun' and that, more-or-less, that is what listeners experienced. Typical was that from *Ultimate Classic Rock*: 'Guitarist Steve Morse gets to employ some different playing techniques, Don Airey rolls out a little barrelhouse piano on some of the tracks and drummer Ian Paice sounds assured in the different rhythmic approaches. Gillan, meanwhile, can sing just about anything, so his voice winds up being the best ambassador for this unlikely fare.'[244]

Commercially, it did not sell as well as recent original albums, but it did okay, appearing quite high up a number of charts, albeit briefly. The Deep Purple of Morse's early days would have killed for even that level of success. Overall, it was a morale booster at the end of a difficult time. The new year — 2022 — promised to be a good one for the band: a new album in the bag, a tour schedule ratcheting up again after all the cancellations, the pandemic receding into the past, even though Covid had not yet been finally conquered...

It was not to be. Within months, one disaster after another would have struck. For Morse personally, the most devastating time of all was coming...

18.
The Loss Inside

Deep Purple convened in Autumn of 2021 to begin work on a new project, but, as Morse later reported, things for him were to go tragically awry: 'I suddenly left the writing session in Germany because my wife was having a real medical crisis.'[245]

He was soon back, playing live with the band for the first time since the lockdowns. In February 2022, they joined a Rock Legends Cruise as part of a bill featuring various big names from the history of pop music.

Those who have followed Deep Purple's career would no doubt find it surprising that they might do anything as apparently uncool as to involve themselves with such an enterprise. Surely, they would not ensconce themselves on a boat for a week providing what was, in effect, the cabaret, would they? Looking more closely at the organisation responsible — the Native American Heritage Association — puts their participation into context.

The stated aim was to raise funds to help alleviate the many problems faced by Native Americans across the USA. In recent years, the years of the pandemic, donations had started to dry up, just as costs had shot through the roof. Coming up with the idea of bringing a few 'legends' together and giving them a guaranteed audience was, in retrospect, a smart move. And the line-up was impressive: when Blue Öyster Cult are present, but not named among the headliners, you have some serious rock firepower on your side.

Given the connection to Native American welfare, it is hard not to detect the hand of Morse in guiding his colleagues towards contributing their talents. This would be a way for him to continue his advocacy in a less low-key way than had hitherto been the case. Unfortunately, three members of the band contracted Covid and so they all had to drop out. It was only the first problem touching on politics that the band faced in the early months of the new year. Another was Russia's invasion of Ukraine.

As an event of global geopolitical significance, it seemed to have little to do with a rock band doing the rounds with their old fashioned sound, but, in the age of Internet-enabled social media, everyone is expected to have not only an opinion, but the correct opinion, and the Internet had decided that Ukraine were the good guys.

In that Deep Purple had associated in the past with Dmitry Medvedev — who may no longer have been Russian President, but still served as deputy chairman of the Security Council of Russia and was among the more hawkish voices backing Vladimir Putin, current President and architect of the war — they could not very well remain silent, as much as they might have wished to.

Their first response was to cancel a concert in Kyiv, which was not a tough decision since the city was being shelled by the Russian army at the time. A similar fate befell a concert planned for Moscow, although that was driven less by safety concerts than a desire to register their disapproval.

The individual members of the band also issued statements. Gillan was typically bullish, sparing Putin no criticisms while lamenting that 'not seeing [their] Russian friends again' would be 'a big sacrifice,' but that this was nothing compared to not seeing their Ukrainian friends who 'are being killed.'[246]

Airey, doubtless to no effect, wrote to Medvedev (did he ever get the letter?) returning an autograph and demanding that one of his be returned to him. As protests go, this is about as close to going through the motions as it is possible to get.

Morse, who had spent his career studiously maintaining an avowedly apolitical stance (his position vis-à-vis Native Americans notwithstanding), gave a measured response: 'As a citizen of a deeply divided country, one thing here that everyone agrees on is: Stop this attack on a country who voluntarily disarmed their nukes to satisfy all the big players. Stop, lower your guns, turn back, help others on the way back!'[247]

But none of this was remotely as important as the personal problems that he and his family were experiencing. Initially, he only planned to take a break. As he wrote in March 2022: 'My dear wife Janine is currently battling cancer. At this point there are so many complications and unknowns that whatever time we have left in our lives; I simply must be there with her.'[248]

He was adamant that he was not leaving the band, but, under the circumstances, could not commit to foreign tours. The Northern Irish guitarist Simon McBride, who had worked with both Airey and Gillan in the past, stepped in as temporary replacement. All pronouncements at this time were at pains to emphasise that Morse remained a permanent member of the band. He talked of returning to the tour as soon as Janine received a 'clean bill of health.'

Yet, the similarities to Jon Lord defiantly proclaiming that a cancer diagnosis would do nothing to slow him down were stark. And, as with Lord, the reality was very different from the rhetoric. By July, it was clear that Morse could not carry on. He was heavily committed to Janine's care, hooking up intravenous drips and taking her to chemotherapy sessions. He was in no position to meet Deep Purple's insatiable demands. His leaving statement gave more detail about his wife's condition: 'We are learning to accept stage 4 aggressive cancer and chemo treatment for the rest of her life.'[249] In that chemo is not a long-term treatment, the subtext was clear. He further confirmed that his final gig with the band had been as part of the Rock Legends Cruise.

There are many disappointing aspects to the manner of his departure. Obviously, the reason for it was utterly devastating. But it is also rather sad that his swan song recording with the band had been *Turning To Crime*, which could charitably be described as 'eccentric,' and that his final live appearance had been as part of a show that — however noble its purpose — had more than a whiff of 'old timers clinging on' about it. But that is how it ended — less with a power chord than a bum note.

Morse was, though, as good as his word and he continued to play music, albeit at venues that were closer to home. He began 2023 by appearing at Joe Satriani's G4, sharing a bill not only with Satriani himself, but Peter Frampton and Steve Lukather among others. It was only an appetiser for dates by a reformed Steve Morse Band, LaRue and Romaine jumping on board with alacrity. Morse was excited by the prospect, saying: 'This mini tour is us getting back to what made us the happiest musically. Working with friends you know and trust, playing snippets of the best parts of your lives together is too much fun to call "work!"'[250]

His choice of words was telling. Would he have said as much about his time with Deep Purple? Interviewed by Pete Pardo some time after the dust had settled, he spoke of the music that he most enjoyed playing: 'My natural inclination and talents and, you know, drawbacks and everything just fit the instrumental — well, the stuff I do with Flying Colors, Dregs and Steve Morse Band. All that fits me — it's an easy fit is what I'm saying. However, I don't think I would have just quit [Deep Purple] because I thought we were going to go a little more — one more album project and tour and be done. I wanted to finish with the band.'[251] He went on to add that McBride, who graduated smoothly to full member status, was closer to the band's sensibilities than he had been.

As for those 'easy fit' projects, they became, at least for a while, more feasible because Janine entered remission. She placed a message on Morse's Facebook page with the news: 'Thought you should all get an update from the "horse's" mouth. I am in remission, no signs of the cancer… just got my chemo port out on Wednesday… Please continue to pray for me though, lots of side effects from the treatments.'[252]

They were not the only danger. As Morse reminded Pardo, cancer is never easily beaten and 'remission' is not synonymous with 'cure' in any context. The symptoms could reappear without warning, necessitating a return to chemo. Hence, the tours were short and the geographical range limited. Morse knew that he might be required to return home at any moment. The workload was closer to what he had always wanted — much to the chagrin of management — even if the reason for it was so awful.

The Steve Morse Band tour had already ended in May 2023 and Morse dropped out of live appearances again for nearly a year. It was a period of highs and lows. Janine's remission was obviously the chief blessing, but, as the year waned and 2024 dawned, it became clear that it was only a respite — and a brief one at that.

On 4th February 2024, at 2:40pm, Janine Morse died.

Morse tells the story of what happened better than anyone else could: 'Anybody who knows the stage 4 cancer treatments, knows that each scan, each blood test is done with fingers crossed. We never knew, but this return of the cancer shocked all our doctors almost as much as us. Just 2 weeks before she died, we were riding around in a small plane, sightseeing several times.'[253]

Morse reported that he saw her in distress as she slept and took a reading of her blood oxygen saturation. Realising that something was not right, he took her immediately to the hospital. Eight days later, she was on full life support with cancer cells ravaging her lungs so quickly and aggressively that chemotherapy was useless.

Perhaps appropriately, the last live event that she and Morse attended, purely as spectators, was headlined by Kansas. Morse requested that any fans who had snapped them both together share their pictures with him. He further spoke movingly of how Janine loved music and travel. He alluded to the support that she had given him at Steve Morse Band gigs. That he was privately distraught was mentioned by Andy West: 'We have had some tough weeks here recently since [Janine] passed away. We all went to her funeral… and that made it much harder and seeing how Steve is suffering.'[254]

This narrative began by imagining a guitarist — Steve Morse — picking up his instrument and beginning to play a song, the song of his life. It's a clumsy metaphor, no doubt, but it has a weight of literary tradition behind it. Here, it might be thought, is the place at which the song ends, with a crash, a crescendo, a few whimsical notes. That would be how an average composer would do it. But Steve Morse has never been an average anything. As with so many of his works over the years, the moment at which the song seems to end is just the start of a whole new phrase, or phase, that could hardly have been predicted when the first few notes hovered delightfully in the air. More was still to come…

Epilogue:
Better Than Walking Away

At bottom, any biography attempts to answer a single, simple question: who is this person? In this case it would be more specifically rendered as, 'who is Steve Morse'? How does one — at the risk of inducing groans — decode Morse?

To call him an enigma would not be quite right. Few, indeed, are the artists and public figures who so readily wear their hearts on their sleeves. His candour and openness at the time of his wife's final illness would not have been so readily forthcoming from many another in his position.

He's not an enigma, then, but maybe he is a paradox. From an early stage of his career, he has routinely been described in interviews, reviews, articles as a 'legend' or 'legendary.' Yet, he has never had a number one hit. He has never had a hit that has even got all that close to number one. He is not followed around by an entourage. He does not need security guards. He frequently appears at events without being readily recognised. For a legend, he is more than a little down-to-earth.

This comes through in his extraordinary generosity with his time. A cursory search of YouTube will uncover hundreds of interviews that he has given, sometimes with obscure fan channels that he must never have thought would do anything much for his public profile. He smiles, answers every question. To be sure, he tends to come across as a little tongue-tied. 'Inarticulate' would be unfair, since his vocabulary, especially regarding music, is broad. But he is apt to wander off into digressions and leave sentences incomplete as a new thought occurs to him. It may be fanciful to say so, but he speaks as he composes. Like his conversation, a typical Steve Morse track — by his own admission — is complicated, non-linear, varying in its moods.

Perhaps it is shyness. It is a rare interview in which he does not hold a guitar and let it do most of the talking for him. His interlocutors on such occasions are surely honoured. Their conversations place into their possession recordings of private performances by Steve Morse, done just for them. As might be expected, he usually plays familiar tunes, but every now and then, something original comes through. It is creativity happening in real time. A testament to his ever-active imagination.

That all having been said, those interviews only seem to be revealing. Morse is happy to discuss himself, but what he does not say is as startling as what he does: almost nothing about his private life, almost nothing about the private lives of his colleagues. When either is mentioned, it is usually only in relation to some story about music. Because, in the end, that is what those interviews are about: music.

So, it comes back to music. It always does. But here again is a paradox. This is a man obsessed with it, who lives for it — but who has given it up more than once. He has stepped back, taken on more everyday occupations. Was he influenced by the Allen Sloans and Andy Wests of this world who managed to successfully juggle steady jobs with occasional forays back into the live scene? Did he see them strike a balance missing from his own life? To some extent, the balance is already there: he has found it in his farm, which is a going concern and a profitable sideline.

The key, though, may be the nature of the jobs he took on during those hiatuses. Practical work. Tough work. As far from the artistry and delicacy of music as it is possible to get. It might be seen as the legacy of a childhood spent in a home that does not seem to have ever been anything other than loving but was one in which music was not highly esteemed. On the other hand, Morse himself would say that it was not music that he quit, but the music business.

To that, he has never fully reconciled himself. His leaving Deep Purple gave a neat cameo of exactly what causes him so much angst. Personally, the band were sad; as Stephen Bentley-Klein had it: 'They're all gentlemen. They all love Steve and no-one wanted him to go.'[255]

Morse's own — more humorous take — was somewhat different: 'I told those guys "I can't do this" and they were upset for like three to four seconds and then moved on.'[256]

He was not accusing them of being cold, simply acknowledging that they, and he, were in a business that does not grant a lot of room for sentimentality. It is next to impossible to get into in the first place and to remain in it, in a prominent place, for fifty or more years — as both Deep Purple and Morse have done — is strictly for the hard-nosed. Someone leaving a band after so long is to be regretted, yes, but not to be dwelt upon: careers beckon and there can be no question of a rethink. What is done is done.

Given what else we know about Morse's personality — his friendliness, his positivity, his obvious love of home and hearth — it is not too surprising that he has shown a marked ambivalence towards the business side of music. He has been fortunate in some respects. Phil Walden and others were happy to indulge him. But more frequent have been the times when he has had forced upon him artistic compromises for the sake of commercial success. Was, as some have argued, his membership of Deep Purple just another compromise?

This depends on the perspective from which he is regarded. If the chosen prism is Deep Purple, he appears as the band's guitarist who happened to get involved with other bands and musicians along the way. If he is viewed in and of himself, however, he comes into focus as a busy musician who spreads his talents widely. Deep Purple were one of his projects, but they were only primus inter pares. His membership of Living Loud, Angelfire, Flying Colors and, naturally, The Steve Morse band and Dixie Dregs, were just as important to him and more representative of his essential nature.

Those projects have ultimately outlived Deep Purple. Less than a month after Janine's passing, he was on the road again, reviving the Dixie Dregs for another tour. The support act? Steve Morse Band. Was he being callous? No. The tour was publicised in 2023, when it was no doubt planned with Janine's blessing. When asked by Pardo whether the setlist would be a 'greatest hits' collection, Morse answered that it would include the expected songs, but he also offered the exciting prospect of new material being tried out ahead of possible new recordings.

The song of Morse's life, then, continues. Maybe by now it's on a long, slow fade — he turned seventy just days before these words were written, but it being his song, it is more than likely a jam. Unpredictable. Creative. Collaborative. Varied. And not as complex as all that. Rather simple, in the final analysis; as simple as practised fingers tripping over taut strings to produce the most beautiful sounds on earth. Sounds that fill the air and rise, floating upwards, turning, undulating, always dynamic, but rising, ever rising, like a plane piloted by a lone aviator (who is also a guitarist) as it disappears into the vast distance of a bright blue clear sky.

Discography

Dixie Dregs
The Great Spectacular (1975)
Free Fall (1977)
What If (1978)
Night Of The Living Dregs (1979)
Dregs Of The Earth (1980)
Unsung Heroes (1981)
Industry Standard (1982)
Off The Record (1988)
Bring 'Em Back Alive   (1992)
Full Circle (1994)
King Biscuit Flower Hour Presents Dixie Dregs (1997)
California Screamin' (2000)
Live At Montreux (1978)   DVD 2005
Live In Connecticut 2001 (+ Cruise Control) (CD / DVD, 2008)
Wages Of Weirdness (2015)

Steve Morse Band and solo*
The Introduction (1984)
Stand Up (1985)
High Tension Wires (1989)
Southern Steel (1991)
Coast To Coast   (1992)
Structural Damage (1995)
StressFest (1996)
Major Impacts (2000)*
Best - Guitar Heroes (2001)
(compilation of tracks by Dixie Dregs, Kansas, Morse, Deep Purple and Lynyrd Skynyrd)
Split Decision (2002)
Major Impacts 2 (2004)*
Prime Cuts Volume (2005)*
Prime Cuts Volume 2 (2005)*
Cruise Control – Live in New York 1992 (CD/DVD, 2008)
Out Standing In Their Field (2009)

Kansas
Power (1986)
In the Spirit of Things (1988)
King Biscuit Flower Hour Presents Kansas (1998)
There's Know Place Like Home (Live   CD/DVD, guest appearance, 2009)

Deep Purple (studio releases)
Purpendicular (1996)
Dick Pimple Present Music From Turtle Island (1996)
(Fan club only release, one ten-minute track, 'Turtle Island Shuffle')
Abandon (1998)
Bananas (2003)
Rapture Of The Deep (2005)
NOW What?! (2013)
InFinite (2017)
Whoosh! (2020)
Turning To Crime (2021)

Deep Purple (live albums)
Live at The Olympia '96 (1997)
Total Abandon Australia '99 (1999)
In Concert with The London Symphony Orchestra (1999)
The Bootleg Series 1984 – 2000 (12 CD box set, Morse on 4 discs, 2000)
Bombay Calling - Deep Purple Live In Bombay '95 (2000)
Around the World 1995 – 1999 (VHS, 2000)
Live At The Rotterdam Ahoy (2001)
The Soundboard Series - Australasian Tour 2001 (12 CD box set, 2001)*
Perihelion   (DVD, 2002)
Live At The NEC (DVD, 2002)
Live Encounters... (CD / DVD, 2004)
Live At Montreux 1996 (2006)
Live At Montreux 2006: They All Came Down To Montreux (2007)
Around The World Live (4 DVD box set, 2008)
Over Zurich (Limited Edition DVD, 2008)
Live At Montreux 2011 (2011)
The NOW What?! Live Tapes (2013)
Celebrating Jon Lord At The Royal Albert Hall (2014)
Live In Verona 2011 (2014)
From The Setting Sun... (in Wacken) (2015)
... To The Rising Sun (in Tokyo) (2015)
The inFinite Live Recordings, Pt. 1 (2017)
Live In Rome 2013 (2019)
Live In London 2002 (2021)
**Most of these concerts have subsequently been released independently of each other.*

Living Loud
Living Loud (2003)
Live in Sydney 2004 (2005)

Mario Fasciano, Steve Morse, Ian Paice, Don Airey
E-Thnik (2005)

Steve Morse & Sarah Spencer
Angelfire (2010)

Flying Colors
Flying Colors (2012)
Live in Europe (2013)
Second Nature (2014)
Second Flight: Live at the Z7 (2015)
Third Degree (2019)
Third Stage: Live in London (2019)
Morsefest 2019 (2019)

Guest appearances, sessions and other releases
Tropical Nights – Liza Minnelli (1977)
Evening Pastoral – Rob Cassels Band (1979)
Schemer-Dreamer – Steve Walsh (1980)
I Wonder How Does Tarzan Shave/Cool In The Movies – Patrick Walsh (1981)
Kamikazee Christian – Rob Cassels Band (1983)
Art In America – Art in America (1983)
The Touch- Sonny Turner (1983)
Storytime – T Lavitz (1986)
Stone From Which The Arch Was Made – Mark O'Connor (1987)
Surveillance – Triumph (1987)
Southern By The Grace Of God – Lynyrd Skynyrd (1988)
Love Your Man – The Rossington Band (1988)
Nashville Rendez-Vous – Marcel Dadi (1990)
Fingers Crossing – Marcel Dadi (1991)
Country Guitar Flavors – Marcel Dadi (1992)
Lone Ranger – Jeff Watson (1992)
Coven, Pitrelli, O'Reilly – CPR (1993)
Thonk – Michael Manring (1994)
Carmine Appice's Guitar Zeus – Carmine Appice (1995)
Signatures – Kevin Crider (1996)
Storm – Torden & Lyn (1997)
Seventh Key – Seventh Key (2001)
Nylon & Steel – Manuel Barrueco (2001)
Feeding the Wheel – Jordan Rudess (2001)
Pavarotti & Friends For Afghanistan – Luciano Pavarotti (2001)
(Smoke On The Water with Deep Purple)
Camino Latino/Latin Journey – Liona Boyd (2002)
Rhythm Of Time – Jordan Rudess (2004)
Guitar Farm – Steve Woolverton (2005)
Gillan's Inn – Ian Gillan (2006)
II – Deacon Street (2006)
School Of The Arts – School Of The Arts (2007)
Porta San Gennaro Napoli – Mario Fasciano / Rick Wakeman / Steve Morse / Ian Paice / Don Airey / Rob Townsend (2008)

Brian Tarquin Presents… Fretworx – Brian Tarquin (2008)
Trading 8s – Carl Verheyen Band (2009)
Classics Anthology – Rob Cassels Band (2009)
Stay Tuned – Bernhard Welz (2011)
Testimony 2 – Neal Morse (2011)
Raised in Captivity – John Wetton (2011)
Guitar Passions – Sharon Isbin & Friends (2011)
Forth – Proto-Kaw (2011)
A Proggy Christmas – The Prog World Orchestra (2012)
The Fusion Syndicate – The Fusion Syndicate (2012)
Concerto For Group And Orchestra – Jon Lord (2012)
Great Gypsy Soul – Tommy Bolin & Friends (2012)
Garrett vs. Paganini – David Garrett (2013)
Epilogue – The Prog Collective (2013)
Caprice- David Garrett (2014)
Guitars For Wounded Warriors – Brian Tarquin & Heavy Friends (2014)
A Song For You (single) – Mario Fasciano / Charlie Cannon / Steve Morse (2014)
tHis is the tHing – Purpendicular (2015)
Citizen- Billy Sherwood (2015)
Don't You Tell Me Not To Play Guitar (single) – Dorian Chiiwahwah Phallic (2016)
Stay Tuned 1.5 – Bernhard Welz (2016)
Band Of Brothers – Brian Tarquin (2017)
Part 1 – Chelsea Constable (2017)
The Mutual Admiration Society – Sterling Ball, John Ferraro & Jim Cox (2018)
Guitars For Veterans – Brian Tarquin & Heavy Friends (2018)
Con Brio – Legacy Pilots (2018)
Stay Tuned (new version) – Bernard Welz (2018)
Triumphant Hearts – Jason Becker (2018)
1000 Hands – Jon Anderson (2019)
All Blues – Peter Frampton (2019)
Vegas Blue - Brian Tarquin (2020)
Sidemen – Sidemen (2020)
Aviation – Legacy Pilots (2020)

Not In Kansas Anymore - A Prog Opera - Robby Steinhardt (2021)

NOTES

Prologue: Here And Now And Then

1 Colin Hart in correspondence with the author.

2 Paul Mann interviewed by the author, 9th December 2022.

3 Pete Pardo in correspondence with the author.

4 Jankowska, L. (2023). Re-thinking virtuosity for the hybrid era of multifarious approaches. Contemporary Music Review, 42(3), 288-303.

5 Stephen Bentley-Klein, interviewed by the author 29th December 2022.

Rising Power

6 Skinner, T. (2022). Deep Purple guitarist Steve Morse officially quits band to care for his ill wife. New Musical Express, 23rd July 2022.

7 Ibid.

8 Ibid.

9 Hett, J. (2014). Interview With Legendary Guitarist Steve Morse (Deep Purple). MusicRecallMagazine. com, https://www.musicrecallmagazine.com/interviews/interview-with-legendary-guitarist-steve-morse/ [accessed Wednesday 21st February 2024].

10 Steve Morse: From The Dregs To Deep Purple and Kansas. Rick Beato, https://youtu.be/_Jxp9k72M1c?si=JAOjGeu9juIVOa2o [accessed Tuesday 27th February 2024].

11 Steve Morse: The Beginning, the End...and Two Resurrections. The Pure Rock Shop, https://tprs.com/interviews/steve-morse/ [accessed Wednesday 21st February 2024].

12 Hett, J. (2014). Interview With Legendary Guitarist Steve Morse (Deep Purple). MusicRecallMagazine. com. https://www.musicrecallmagazine.com/interviews/interview-with-legendary-guitarist-steve-morse/ [accessed Wednesday 21st February 2024].

13 Steve Morse: The Beginning, the End...and Two Resurrections. The Pure Rock Shop, https://tprs.com/interviews/steve-morse/ [accessed Saturday 2nd March 2024].

14 Frederick, J. (2017). The persistent South: Southern distinctiveness, cultural identity and change. Proceedings of the 8th International Scientific Forum, September 2017, UNCP, USA.

15 Obrecht, J. (2023). Steve Morse: The Complete 1978 Dixie Dregs Interview (HD Audio). Talking Guitar, https://jasobrecht.substack.com/p/steve-morse-the-complete-1978-dixie [accessed Saturday 2nd March 2024].

16 Hett, J. (2014). Interview With Legendary Guitarist Steve Morse (Deep Purple). MusicRecallMagazine. com. https://www.musicrecallmagazine.com/interviews/interview-with-legendary-guitarist-steve-morse/ [accessed Wednesday 28th February 2024].

17 Obrecht, J. (2023). Steve Morse: The Complete 1978 Dixie Dregs Interview (HD Audio). Talking Guitar, https://jasobrecht.substack.com/p/steve-morse-the-complete-1978-dixie [accessed Sunday 3rd March 2024].

18 Johnson, K. (2018). Dawn of the Dregs: An Interview With Andy West. No Treble, https://www.notreble.com/buzz/2018/01/19/dawn-of-the-dregs-an-interview-with-andy-west/ [accessed Saturday 2nd March 2024].

19 Hett, J. (2014). Interview With Legendary Guitarist Steve Morse (Deep Purple). MusicRecallMagazine. com. https://www.musicrecallmagazine.com/interviews/interview-with-legendary-guitarist-steve-morse/ [accessed Saturday 2nd March 2024].

20 Ferguson, K. (1994). A talk with Steve Morse. The Highway Star, https://www.thehighwaystar.com/rosas/morse/SM-interv.html [accessed Wednesday 10th April 2024].

21 Obrecht, J. (2023). Steve Morse: The Complete 1978 Dixie Dregs Interview (HD Audio). Talking Guitar, https://jasobrecht.substack.com/p/steve-morse-the-complete-1978-dixie [accessed Saturday 20th April 2024].

Name Dropping

22 Green, L. (2002). How Popular Musicians Learn: A Way Ahead for Music Education. Ashgate.

23 Pete Hook on the DVD commentary to the film '24 Hour Party People'.

24 Straw, W. (1984). Characterizing rock music cultures: The case of heavy metal. Canadian University Music Review, 5, 104-122.

25 Sharman, L. & Dingle, G. A. (2015). Extreme metal music and danger processing. Frontiers in Human Neuroscience, 9.

26 McAvinchey, D, (n.d.). Influences: Steve Morse. Guitar Nine, https://www.guitar9.com/column/influences-steve-morse [accessed Thursday 4th April 2024].

27 Eichaan (2018). Appreciating Hiram Bullock. TDPRI.com, https://www.tdpri.com/threads/appreciating-hiram-bullock.880719/ [accessed Wednesday 10th April 2024].

28 McAvinchey, D, (n.d.). Influences: Steve Morse. Guitar Nine, https://www.guitar9.com/column/influences-steve-morse [accessed Thursday 4th April 2024].

29 Eichaan (2018). Appreciating Hiram Bullock. TDPRI.com, https://www.tdpri.com/threads/appreciating-hiram-bullock.880719/ [accessed Wednesday 10th April 2024].

30 Obrecht, J. (2023). Steve Morse: The Complete 1978 Dixie Dregs Interview (HD Audio). Talking Guitar, https://jasobrecht.substack.com/p/steve-morse-the-complete-1978-dixie [accessed Saturday 20th April 2024].

31 Last.fm: Steve Morse, https://www.last.fm/music/Steve+Morse/+wiki [accessed Wednesday 28th February 2024].

32 Steve Morse. Last.fm, https://www.last.fm/music/Steve+Morse/+wiki [accessed Tuesday 10th April 2024].

33 Johnson, K. (2018). Dawn of the Dregs: An Interview With Andy West. No Treble, https://www.notreble.com/buzz/2018/01/19/dawn-of-the-dregs-an-interview-with-andy-west/ [accessed Saturday 2nd March 2024].

34 Ibid.

35 Prasad, A. (2020). Steve Morse: Spirit Core. Innerviews, https://www.innerviews.org/inner/steve-morse [accessed Tuesday 9th April 2024].

Out Standing In Their Field

36 A moment in rock history- how the Dixie Dregs were discovered. Irocku, https://www.irocku.com/dixie-dregs/ [accessed Saturday 20th April 2024].

37 Obrecht, J. (2023). Steve Morse: The Complete 1978 Dixie Dregs Interview (HD Audio). Talking Guitar, https://jasobrecht.substack.com/p/steve-morse-the-complete-1978-dixie [accessed Sunday 21st April 2024].

38 Dixie Dregs Concert Setlists and Tour Dates. Setlist.fm, https://www.setlist.fm/setlists/dixie-dregs-63d6aa73.html?page=27 [accessed Saturday 27th April 2024].

39 Edgers, P. (2017). Eclectic style, in music and in life. Citizen Times, https://eu.citizen-times.com/story/news/madison/2017/03/15/eclectic-style-music-and-life/99017766/ [accessed Saturday 27th April 2024].

40 Ibid.

41 Meredith, B. (2024). The experimental journey of The Dixie Dregs. Palm Beach Arts Paper, http://palmbeachartspaper.com/the-experimental-journey-of-the-dixie-dregs/ [accessed Sunday 28th April 2024].

42 Obrecht, J. (2023). Steve Morse: The Complete 1978 Dixie Dregs Interview (HD Audio). Talking Guitar, https://jasobrecht.substack.com/p/steve-morse-the-complete-1978-dixie [accessed Sunday 21st April 2024].

43 Meredith, B. (2024). The experimental journey of The Dixie Dregs. Palm Beach Arts Paper, http://palmbeachartspaper.com/the-experimental-journey-of-the-dixie-dregs/ [accessed Sunday 28th April 2024].

44 Ibid.

45 Obrecht, J. (2023). Steve Morse: The Complete 1978 Dixie Dregs Interview (HD Audio). Talking Guitar, https://jasobrecht.substack.com/p/steve-morse-the-complete-1978-dixie [accessed Sunday 21st April 2024].

46 Radz, M. (1979). A subtle hand grenade. The Montreal Star, Friday 20th April 1979.

47 Locey, B. (1992). Classic Eclectic. The Los Angeles Times, Thursday 12th November 1992.

48 Fink, J. (2023). Capricorn Records: The rise and drug-addled fall of the label that launched Southern Rock. Spin.com, https://www.spin.com/2023/01/capricorn-records-rise-fall-southern-rock/ [accessed Tuesday, 30th April 2024].

49 King, B. (1981). Phil Walden talks tall on the comeback trail. The Atlanta Journal, Saturday 30th May 1981.

50 Wosala, S. (1981). In the groove. Messenger-Press, Thursday 25th June 1981.

51 Ibid.

Just Out Of Reach

52 Paul, A. (2014). Organisation man – Twiggs Lyndon's wild life and eerie death. Alanpaul.net, http://alanpaul.net/2017/11/organization-man-twiggs-lyndons-wild-life-and-eerie-death/ [accessed Friday, 3rd May 2024].

53 Wosala, S. (1981). In the groove. Messenger-Press, Thursday 25th June 1981.

54 Prasad, A. (2020). Steve Morse: Spirit Core. Innerviews, https://www.innerviews.org/inner/steve-morse [accessed Tuesday 9th April 2024].

55 Cain, S. (1981). Atlanta-based Dregs keeps Dixie in its act. The Atlanta Journal, Friday 24th April 1981.

56 Feldman, M. (1982). Mark O'Connor: From the Dawgs to the Dregs. Downbeat: The Contemporary Music Magazine, 49(6), 16-18.

57 Ibid.

58 Kopp, B. (2018). Dixie Dregs answer the question: 'What if?' Stomp and Stammer, https://stompandstammer.com/feature-stories/dixie-dregs/#:~:text=In%20later%20years%2C%20the%20band,after%201982's%20Industry%20Standard%20LP.

59 Prasad, A. (2020). Steve Morse: Spirit Core. Innerviews, https://www.innerviews.org/inner/steve-morse [accessed Tuesday 9th April 2024].

60 The Greenville News, Friday 3rd June, 1983.

61 Pete Pardo in correspondence with the author.

62 Ibid

63 Aardschok Magazine (1996). Interview with Steve Morse. The Highway Star, https://www.thehighwaystar.com/rosas/morse/aardmint.htm [accessed Monday 20th May 2024].

Tumeni Notes

64 Steve Morse. Last.fm, https://www.last.fm/music/Steve+Morse/+wiki [accessed Tuesday 10th April 2024].

65 Morse, S. (1986). Open Ears: On The Road With Rush. Guitar for the Practicing Musician, August 1986.

66 Steve Morse: The Beginning, the End…and Two Resurrections. The Pure Rock Shop, https://tprs.com/interviews/steve-morse/ [accessed Saturday 2nd March 2024].

67 Ibid.

68 Ibid.

69 Bosso, J. (2009). 7 career defining records of Steve Morse. Musicradar, https://www.musicradar.com/news/guitars/7-career-defining-records-of-steve-morse-216072 [accessed Thursday 9th May 2024].

70 The Greenville News, Friday 3rd June 1983.

71 Clark, L. (1985). December concert scene begins with a heated rush. The Kennebec Journal, Friday 13th December 1985.

72 Steve Morse: The Beginning, the End…and Two Resurrections. The Pure Rock Shop, https://tprs.com/interviews/steve-morse/ [accessed Saturday 2nd March 2024].

Arena Rock

73 Kielty, M. (2023). Kansas' Rich Williams feared Steve Morse's arrival. Ultimate Classic Rock, https://ultimateclassicrock.com/rich-williams-kansas-steve-morse/ [accessed Monday 20th May 2024].

74 Steve Morse of Deep Purple: Interview from 2000. Outsider Rock, https://outsiderrock.ca/2018/08/27/steve-morse-of-deep-purple-interview-from-2000/ [accessed Monday 20th May 2024].

75 Marymont, M. (1987). New Kansas features 'old' Steve Walsh. Springfield Leader and Press, Thursday 19th February 1987.

76 Tessier, D. (1990). Steve Morse rocks hard, works hard. Albuquerque Journal, Friday 2nd February 1990.

77 Billboard, November 1st, 1986.

78 Setlist.fm, https://www.setlist.fm/setlist/kansas/1987/riverside-theater-milwaukee-wi-bc1c5ca.html [accessed Thursday 23rd May 2024].

79 Kielty, M. (2023). Kansas' Rich Williams feared Steve Morse's arrival. Ultimate Classic Rock, https://ultimateclassicrock.com/rich-williams-kansas-steve-morse/ [accessed Monday 20th May 2024].

80 Prasad, A. (1992). Steve Morse: Unsung hero. Innerviews, https://www.innerviews.org/inner/morse-1 [accessed Saturday 25th May 2024].

81 Heckman, D. (1992). Steve Morse Soars in 2 Different Crafts : Music: Guitarist, who was once a commercial pilot, says flying helps his work, allowing him to see the big picture. LA Times, August 29th 1992.

82 MeTV (2023). Interview with Billy Greer, https://metv.com/stories/carry-on-dust-in-the-wind-and-bob-ezrin-pt-3-of-our-billy-greer-interview [accessed Friday 24th May 2024.

83 Ibid.

84 Interview with Richard Williams (Kansas). DMME.net, https://dmme.net/interviews/interview-with-richard-williams-kansas [accessed Friday 24th May 2024].

85 Prasad, A. (2020). Steve Morse: Spirit Core. Innerviews, https://www.innerviews.org/inner/steve-morse [accessed Tuesday 9th April 2024].

86 McTavish, B. (1989). The state of their union. The Kansas City Star, Friday 20th January 1989.

87 The Daily Illini, Friday 21st October 1988.

88 The Gazette, Thursday 26th January, 1989.

89 Erlewine, S. (n.d.) AllMusic review of 'In the Spirit of Things' by Kansas, https://www.allmusic.com/album/in-the-spirit-of-things-mw0000652714 [accessed Saturday 25th May 2024].

The Road Home

90 Borg, J. (2024). Steve Morse quit music to become an airline pilot – until Lynyrd Skynyrd persuaded him to return. Guitar World.

91 Ibid.

92 Ibid.

93 Prasad, A. (1991). Steve Morse: Collaborative departures. Innerviews, https://www.innerviews.org/inner/morse-2 [accessed Saturday 25th May 2024].

94 Ibid.

95 Prasad, A. (1992). Steve Morse: Unsung hero. Innerviews, https://www.innerviews.org/inner/morse-1 [accessed Saturday 25th May 2024].

96 Ibid.

97 Musicians having coffee and talking about stuff – Episode 13: Steve Morse, https://youtu.be/okFrdoX_6Vw?si=GGdfMGZm56QodCY5 [accessed Tuesday 2nd July 2024].

98 Prasad, A. (1992). Steve Morse: Unsung hero. Innerviews, https://www.innerviews.org/inner/morse-1 [accessed Saturday 25th May 2024].

99 Gioffre, D. (n.d.). AllMusic review of 'Coast to Coast' by Steve Morse Band, https://www.allmusic.com/album/coast-to-coast-mw0000077758#:~:text=AllMusic%20Review&text=From%20classical%20guitar%20to%20guitar,lot%20into%20each%20of%20them. [accessed Sunday 26th May 2024].

100 Prasad, A. (1991). Steve Morse: Collaborative departures. Innerviews, https://www.innerviews.org/inner/morse-2 [accessed Saturday 25th May 2024].

101 Prasad, A. (1992). Steve Morse: Unsung hero. Innerviews, https://www.innerviews.org/inner/morse-1 [accessed Saturday 25th May 2024].

102 New Jerry Goodman Interview- On Mahavishnu, Dixie Dregs, and more! Progressive Ears, https://www.progressiveears.org/forum/showthread.php/27043-New-Jerry-Goodman-Interview-On-Mahavishnu-Dixie-Dregs-and-more! [accessed Wednesday 29th May 2024].

103 Woodard, J. (1994). Rock Band Out of Past, but With a Difference : Dixie Dregs have always followed their own musical path and kept loyal listeners. They play at Ventura Theatre Tuesday. Los Angeles Times, July 14th 1994.

104 Edmonds, B. (1994). Review of 'Full Circle' by Dixie Dregs. Detroit Free Press, Saturday 25th June 1994.

105 Woodard, J. (1994). Rock Band Out of Past, but With a Difference : Dixie Dregs have always followed their own musical path and kept loyal listeners. They play at Ventura Theatre Tuesday. Los Angeles Times, July 14th 1994.

106 Ibid.

107 Ramstetter, M. (1994). Over the weekend. The Buffalo News, Monday 27th June 1994.

108 Prasad, A. (2020). Steve Morse: Spirit Core. Innerviews, https://www.innerviews.org/inner/steve-morse [accessed Tuesday 9th April 2024].

The Purpendicular Waltz

109 Colin Hart in correspondence with the author.

110 Steve Morse interview: Joining Deep Purple, iGuitar Magazine Issue 9, https://youtu.be/jm7p4zz9Lng?si=XOnGi1pgESlrznw9 [accessed Saturday 1st June 2024].

111 Ibid.

112 Colin Hart in correspondence with the author

113 Ibid.

114 Ibid.

115 Ibid.

116 Steve Morse interviewed by Jerry Bloom, December 9th 2004

117 Aardschok Magazine (1996). Interview with Steve Morse. The Highway Star, https://www.thehighwaystar.com/rosas/morse/aardmint.htm [accessed Monday 20th May 2024].

118 Ibid.

119 Steve Morse Band 'Stressfest' review. The Record, Friday 10th January 1997.

120 Prasad, A. (2020). Steve Morse: Spirit Core. Innerviews, https://www.innerviews.org/inner/steve-morse [accessed Tuesday 9th April 2024].

121 Voter, M. (1996). Perfect Stranger. Asbury Park Press, Sunday 24th November 1996.

122 Ibid.

123 Aardschok Magazine (1996). Interview with Steve Morse. The Highway Star, https://www.thehighwaystar.com/rosas/morse/aardmint.htm [accessed Monday 20th May 2024].

Fingers To The Bone

124 Diaz, J. (1997). A bad night in Santiago. The Highway Star, https://www.thehighwaystar.com/reviews/samerica/chile.html [accessed Tuesday 4th June 2024].

125 8 reasons why Steve Morse was the perfect Deep Purple guitarist. Ultimate Guitar.com, https://www.ultimate-guitar.com/articles/features/8_reasons_why_steve_morse_was_the_perfect_deep_purple_guitarist-136412 [accessed Wednesday 5th June 2024].

126 Review of Deep Purple 'Abandon'. The Birmingham Post, Saturday 4th July 1998.

127 Steve Morse of Deep Purple: Interview from 2000. Outsider Rock, https://outsiderrock.ca/2018/08/27/steve-morse-of-deep-purple-interview-from-2000/ [accessed Monday 20th May 2024].

128 Steve Morse: The Beginning, the End…and Two Resurrections. The Pure Rock Shop, https://tprs.com/interviews/steve-morse/ [accessed Saturday 2nd March 2024].

129 O'Leary, G. (2000). Deep Purple survives turmoil. Sentinel Tribune, Thursday 8th June 2000.

130 Steve Morse on Something Else! The Highway Star, https://www.thehighwaystar.com/news/2013/05/16/5838/ [accessed Saturday 8th June 2024].

131 Steve Morse remembers Jon. Jon Lord Official Website, https://jonlord.org/2013/05/01/steve-morse-remembers-jon/ [accessed Saturday 8th June 2024].

132 8 reasons why Steve Morse was the perfect Deep Purple guitarist. Ultimate Guitar.com, https://www.ultimate-guitar.com/articles/features/8_reasons_why_steve_morse_was_the_perfect_deep_purple_guitarist-136412 [accessed Wednesday 5th June 2024].

133 Paul Mann interviewed by the author, 9th December 2022.

134 Steve Morse, 'Major Impacts'. Guitar Nine, https://www.guitar9.com/column/steve-morse-major-impacts [accessed Saturday 8th June 2024].

135 Bumgardner, E. (2000). Review of Steve Morse, 'Major Impacts'. The Daily Progress, Friday 11th August 2000.

136 Paul Mann interviewed by the author, 9th December 2022.

137 De Yampert, R. (n.d.). Guitarist Steve Morse plays the bank. Daytona Beach News Journal, https://eu.news-journalonline.com/story/news/2015/05/12/guitarist-steve-morse-plays-the-bank/30715858007/ [accessed Monday 10th June 2024].

Structural Damage

138 Bowden, M. (2003). Steve Morse Band: Split Decision. Popmatters.com, https://www.popmatters.com/morsesteveband-split-2495991503.html [accessed Tuesday 11th June 2024].

139 Steve Morse: The Beginning, the End...and Two Resurrections. The Pure Rock Shop, https://tprs.com/interviews/steve-morse/ [accessed Saturday 2nd March 2024].

140 Steve Morse interviewed by Pete Pardo. Sea of Tranquility, https://youtu.be/vyPCoPjDpWg?si=2bVoGIAce6LU5B_L [accessed Wednesday 12th June 2024].

141 Steve Morse interviewed by Jerry Bloom, 9th December 2004.

142 Benson, J. (2003). Review of Deep Purple 'Bananas'. The News Journal, Thursday 6th November 2003.

143 Florida Today review of Deep Purple 'Bananas', Friday 10th October 2003.

144 Steve Morse interviewed by Jerry Bloom, 9th December 2004.

145 Letter from Ian Gillan. The Highway Star, https://www.thehighwaystar.com/news/news03-042005.html [accessed Thursday 13th June 2024].

146 Steve Morse interviewed by Jerry Bloom, 9th December 2004.

147 Ibid.

148 Ibid.

149 Ibid.

150 Don Airey talks about Living Loud, joining Deep Purple. Blabbermouth.net, https://blabbermouth.net/news/don-airey-talks-about-living-loud-joining-deep-purple [accessed Saturday 15th June 2024].

151 Living Loud Documentary 2004, https://youtu.be/CUvz7H2Bpdc?si=QyIJ6K9MVRdWuGlw [accessed Saturday 15th

152 Steve Morse interviewed by Jerry Bloom, 9th December 2004.

153 Ibid.

Slice Of Time

154 Brioux, B. (2005). Live 8 creaks like old baby boomer's knees. The Winnipeg Sun, Saturday 26th June 2005.

155 Deep-Purple.net, https://www.deep-purple.net/review/rapture/rapture-epk.htm [accessed Monday 17th June 2024].

156 Review of Deep Purple, 'Rapture of the Deep'. The Winnipeg Sun, Friday 25th November 2005

157 Review of Deep Purple, 'Rapture of the Deep'. BBC Music, https://www.bbc.co.uk/music/reviews/wnjw [accessed Monday 17th June 2024].

158 Deep Purple guitarist answers fan questions. Blabbermouth.net, https://blabbermouth.net/news/deep-purple-guitarist-answers-fan-questions [accessed Tuesday 18th June 2024].

159 Wright, J. (n.d). Steve Morse: Flying high again. Classic Rock Revisited, https://www.classicrockrevisited.com/show_interview.php?id=134 [accessed Tuesday 18th June 2024].

160 Ibid

161 Steve Morse interviewed by Jerry Bloom, 9th December 2004.

162 Patterson, I. (2008). T. Lavitz: Back to School. All About Jazz, https://www.allaboutjazz.com/t-lavitz-back-to-school-t-lavitz-by-ian-patterson [accessed Saturday 29th June 2024].

163 Prasad, A. (2020). Steve Morse: Spirit Core. Innerviews, https://www.innerviews.org/inner/steve-morse [accessed Tuesday 9th April 2024].

164 Steve Morse releases new vocal album, 'Angelfire'. The Highway Star, https://www.thehighwaystar.com/news/2010/07/14/steve-morse-releases-new-vocal-album-angelfire/ [accessed Wednesday 19th June 2024].

165 Sarah Spencer interview. Musical Discoveries, https://musicaldiscoveries.com/reviews/sarahspencer.htm [accessed Wednesday 19th June 2024].

Brave New World

166 Russia's likely next president met with Deep Purple. Kyiv Post, 12th February 2008.

167 Bienstock, R. (2013). Purple Heart: Daredevil Guitar Virtuoso Steve Morse Discusses Deep Purple's New Album, 'Now What?!' Guitar World, https://www.guitarworld.com/features/purple-heart-daredevil-guitar-virtuoso-steve-morse-discusses-deep-purples-new-album-now-what [accessed Thursday 20th June 2024].

168 Tuttle, E. (2009). When I listen to every song without skipping tracks, I know I've got a keeper. Sun-Journal, Wednesday 25th November 2009.

169 Krueger, A. (2005). The economics of real superstars: The market for rock concerts in the material world. Journal of Labour Economics, 23(1), 1-30.

170 Bienstock, R. (2013). Purple Heart: Daredevil Guitar Virtuoso Steve Morse Discusses Deep Purple's New Album, 'Now What?!' Guitar World, https://www.guitarworld.com/features/purple-heart-daredevil-guitar-virtuoso-steve-morse-discusses-deep-purples-new-album-now-what [accessed Thursday 20th June 2024].

171 The Daily Herald-Tribune, Thursday 24th March 2011.

172 Jomatami (2020). Don Airey recalls problems he faced in Deep Purple after replacing Jon Lord. Ultimate Guitar.com, https://www.ultimate-guitar.com/news/general_music_news/don_airey_recalls_problems_he_faced_in_deep_purple_after_replacing_jon_lord_talks_major_difference_from_the_rolling_stones.html [accessed Saturday 22nd June, 2024].

173 Prasad, A. (2020). Steve Morse: Spirit Core. Innerviews, https://www.innerviews.org/inner/steve-morse [accessed Tuesday 9th April 2024].

The Great Spectacular

174 Steve Morse in the Birmingham Post. The Highway Star, https://www.thehighwaystar.com/news/2009/09/28/steve-morse-in-the-birmingham-post/ [accessed Tuesday 27th December 2022].

175 Stephen Bentley-Klein, interviewed by the author 29th December 2022.

176 Erickson, A. (2011). Deep Purple's Steve Morse: 2011 Symphonic Tour, 'Isn't Going to be Orchestra-Based.' Ultimate Classic Rock, https://ultimateclassicrock.com/deep-purple-2011-orchestra-tour-steve-morse-interview/ [accessed Tuesday 27th December 2022].

177 Tedaldi, J. (2011). Steve Morse interviews April/June 2011. Darker Than Blue, https://darkerthanblue.wordpress.com/interviews/steve-morse-interviews-april-june-2011/#:~:text=Is%20this%20going%20to%20be,arrangements%20with%20horns%20and%20strings. [accessed Sunday 23rd June 2024].

178 Stephen Bentley-Klein, interviewed by the author 29th December 2022.

179 Perry, W. (2011). Review of Deep Purple with Orchestra, Live at Montreux. Democrat and Chronicle, Friday 6th January 2012.

180 Ling, D. (2023). An introduction to Flying Colors. Loudersound.com, https://www.loudersound.com/features/an-introduction-to-flying-colors [accessed Wednesday 26th June 2024].

181 Ibid.

182 Ibid.

183 Ibid.

184 Musicians having coffee and talking about stuff – Episode 13: Steve Morse, https://youtu.be/okFrdoX_6Vw?si=GGdfMGZm56QodCY5 [accessed Tuesday 2nd July 2024].

185 Ibid.

186 Ling, D. (2023). An introduction to Flying Colors. Loudersound.com, https://www.loudersound.com/features/an-introduction-to-flying-colors [accessed Wednesday 26th June 2024].

187 Flying Colors (Steve Morse) interview. Stroppy Baby, https://stroppybaby.com.au/flying-colors-steve-morse-interview/ [accessed Sunday 30th June 2024].

188 Paul Mann interviewed by the author, 9th December 2022.

189 Steve Morse on Something Else! The Highway Star, https://www.thehighwaystar.com/news/2013/05/16/5838/ [accessed Saturday 8th June 2024].

190 Deep Purple guitarist Steve Morse pays tribute to Jon Lord. Blabbermouth.net, https://blabbermouth.net/news/deep-purple-guitarist-steve-morse-pays-tribute-to-jon-lord [accessed Wednesday 26th June 2024].

191 Ibid.

192 Morse is 'still sort of like a music fan'. The Highway Star, https://www.thehighwaystar.com/news/2012/05/02/morse-is-still-sort-of-like-a-music-fan/ [accessed Sunday 30th June 2024].

193 Joe Satriani Universe, https://www.joesatrianiuniverse.com/g3/ [accessed Thursday 4th July 2024].

194 Mathias, G. L. (2014). Flying Colors – Steve Morse – Interview @ Islington Town Hall, London, UK. Riff Metal Mag, https://archive.ph/20141130051253/http://www.riff-mag.com/2014/11/03/flying-colors-steve-morse-interview-islington-town-hall-london-uk/ [accessed Thursday 4th July 2024].

Uncommon Man

195 Producer Bob Ezrin helps Deep Purple channel its past with NOW What?! Goldmine, https://www.goldminemag.com/articles/deep-purple-channels-past-help-producer-bob-ezrin [accessed Tuesday 3rd January 2023].

196 Ibid.

197 Hett, J. (2014). Interview With Legendary Guitarist Steve Morse (Deep Purple). MusicRecallMagazine.com, https://www.musicrecallmagazine.com/interviews/interview-with-legendary-guitarist-steve-morse/ [accessed Wednesday 21st February 2024].

198 Prasad, A. (2020). Steve Morse: Spirit Core. Innerviews, https://www.innerviews.org/inner/steve-morse [accessed Tuesday 9th April 2024].

199 Bienstock, R. (2013). Purple Heart: Daredevil Guitar Virtuoso Steve Morse Discusses Deep Purple's New Album, 'Now What?!' Guitar World, https://www.guitarworld.com/features/purple-heart-daredevil-guitar-virtuoso-steve-morse-discusses-deep-purples-new-album-now-what [accessed Thursday 20th June 2024].

200 Derrough, L. M. (n.d.) Steve Morse – Deep Purple and Flying Colors (INTERVIEW). Glide Magazine, https://glidemagazine.com/20603/steve-morse-deep-purple-and-flying-colors/ [accessed Sunday 30th June 2024].

201 Derrough, L. M. (n.d.) Steve Morse – Deep Purple and Flying Colors (INTERVIEW). Glide Magazine, https://glidemagazine.com/20603/steve-morse-deep-purple-and-flying-colors/ [accessed Sunday 30th June 2024].

202 Flying Colors (Steve Morse) interview. Stroppy Baby, https://stroppybaby.com.au/flying-colors-steve-morse-interview/ [accessed Sunday 30th June 2024].

203 Review of Flying Colors Live in Europe. Classic Rock Revisited, https://www.classicrockrevisited.com/show_review.php?id=1184 [accessed Sunday 30th June 2024].

204 Barton, G. (2014). Interview: Ian Paice on the Jon Lord tribute show. Classic Rock.

205 Darker Than Blue, Jon Lord Memorial Concert review.

Collateral Damage

206 Prasad, A. (2020). Steve Morse: Spirit Core. Innerviews, https://www.innerviews.org/inner/steve-morse [accessed Tuesday 9th April 2024].

207 Jomatami (2020). Deep Purple's Steve Morse explains how unusual picking gave him exceptional clarity, but damaged his hands. Ultimate Guitar.com, https://www.ultimate-guitar.com/news/general_music_news/deep_purples_steve_morse_explains_how_unusual_picking_style_gave_him_exceptional_clarity_but_damaged_his_hands.html [accessed Tuesday 2nd July 2024].

208 Kielty, M. (2014). Flying Colors premiere Mask Machine. Classic Rock.

209 Mathias, G. L. (2014). Flying Colors – Steve Morse – Interview @ Islington Town Hall, London, UK. Riff Metal Mag, https://archive.ph/20141130051253/http://www.riff-mag.com/2014/11/03/flying-colors-steve-morse-interview-islington-town-hall-london-uk/ [accessed Thursday 4th July 2024].

210 Steve Morse from Flying Colors talks about new album Second Nature, guitargodstv, https://youtu.be/cK9QetxLXk0?si=n3wxrQN1pXf06DAZ

211 Mathias, G. L. (2014). Flying Colors – Steve Morse – Interview @ Islington Town Hall, London, UK. Riff Metal Mag, https://archive.ph/20141130051253/http://www.riff-mag.com/2014/11/03/flying-colors-steve-morse-interview-islington-town-hall-london-uk/ [accessed Thursday 4th July 2024].

212 Ibid

213 Review of 'Second Nature' by Flying Colors. The Day, Thursday 11th December 2014.

214 Jon Lord interviewed by Jerry Bloom, 21st November 2007.

215 Colothan, S. (2017). Deep Purple's Steve Morse on Ritchie Blackmore reunion: 'It would be nice to see closure.' Planet Rock, https://hellorayo.co.uk/planet-rock/news/rock-news/deep-purples-steve-morse-on-ritchie-blackmore-reunion-it-would-be-nice-to-see-closure/ [accessed Saturday 6th July 2024].

216 David Garrett: Most sincere interview. Best of Baltic Entertainment, https://youtu.be/oGBBQ4tbmCI?si=2CKhE5cEgRx7oDm_

217 Flying Colors – 'Second Flight: Live at the Z7'. The Prog Mind, https://theprogmind.com/2015/11/05/flying-colors-second-flight-live-at-the-z7/ [accessed Sunday 7th July 2024].

218 Ibid.

219 Arvia, P. (2016). Halls of fame are not needed for validation. Chicago Tribune, Tuesday 19th April 2016.

Shoulda Coulda Woulda

220 Deep Purple's Ian Gillan on the rock and roll hall of fame: 'There are some people that decided The Monkees were America's answer to The Beatles' Noise creep, https://noisecreep.com/deep-purple-rock-and-roll-hall-of-fame/ [accessed Sunday 22nd January 2023].

221 Greene, A. (2016). Deep Purple guitarist Ritchie Blackmore won't attend Hall of Fame ceremony. Rolling Stone,19th February 2016.

222 The Phoenician (2022). 8 reasons why Steve Morse was the perfect Deep Purple guitarist. Ultimate Guitar, https://www.ultimate-guitar.com/articles/features/8_reasons_why_steve_morse_was_the_perfect_deep_purple_guitarist-136412 [accessed Thursday 1st August 2024].

223 Parry, W. (2017). Deep Purple digs deep for classic sound on new album. Bristol Herald Courier, Sunday 16th April 2017.

224 Lester, P. (2017). Deep Purple – InFinite album review. Classic Rock, 27th February 2017.

225 Why Deep Purple named their tour The Long Goodbye. Ultimate Classic Rock, https://ultimateclassicrock.com/deep-purple-long-goodbye-tour-2/ [accessed Sunday 29th January 2023].

226 Magnotta, A. (2018). Steve Morse doubts Deep Purple members are truly retiring. Q104.3, https://q1043.iheart.com/featured/ken-dashow/content/2018-06-07-steve-morse-doubts-deep-purple-members-are-truly-retiring/ [accessed Sunday 4th August 2024].

227 Rod Morgenstein reunion promo for Rock, Roots and Blues – Live, https://youtube.com/shorts/GA3-UxpHdok?si=tJdxQLNZaDF73dFL

228 The Des Moines Register, Saturday 7th April 2018.

229 Dixie Dregs interview with bassist Andy West 2018 JAM Magazine, https://youtu.be/NzZe-zsQkHM?si=TtwNmnhXjTwCSLKk

230 Prasad, A. (2020). Steve Morse: Spirit Core. Innerviews, https://www.innerviews.org/inner/steve-morse [accessed Tuesday 9th April 2024].

231 Ibid

232 Condran, E. (2018). For the first time in 40 years, the original Dixie Dregs are back on stage together. The News and Observer, Friday 2nd March 2018.

233 Cox, A. (2018). Dixie Dregs at The Boulder Theater, Denver, Colorado (April 14th, 2018), Sonic Perspectives, https://www.sonicperspectives.com/concert-reviews/dixie-dregs-april-2018/?utm_content=cmp-true [accessed Thursday 8th August 2024].

234 The Arizona Republic, Sunday 22nd April 2018.

Clearly Quite Absurd

235 Liebman, J. (2019). Dave LaRue interview. For Bass Players Only, https://forbassplayersonly.com/dave-larue-interview/ [accessed Saturday 10th August 2024].

236 Vol. 102 Steve Morse / October 2019. Muse on Muse, https://www.museonmuse.jp/?p=10623 [accessed Sunday 11th August 2024].

237 Review: Flying Colors 'Third Degree'. Sea of Tranquility, https://youtu.be/SNsSeoHVYSg?si=V48ochneFPxFyT7-

238 Flying Colors 'Third Degree' album review. The Prog Report, https://progreport.com/flying-colors-third-degree-album-review/

239 Deep Purple's lockdown was a 'dress rehearsal for retirement'. Ultimate Classic Rock, https://ultimateclassicrock.com/deep-purple-retirement/ [accessed Wednesday 1st February 2023].

240 Brannigan, P. (2021). How Deep Purple turned to crime. Classic Rock, 21st December 2021.

241 Ryan, J. (2021). Roger Glover on new Deep Purple album 'Turning to Crime'. Forbes, https://www.forbes.com/sites/jimryan1/2021/11/26/roger-glover-on-new-deep-purple-album-turning-to-crime/ [accessed Friday 16th August 2024].

242 Steve Morse interview with Six String Alliance, December 28th 2021.

243 Ibid.

244 Review of Deep Purple 'Turning to Crime'. Ultimate Classic Rock, https://ultimateclassicrock.com/deep-purple-turning-to-crime-album-review/?utm_source=tsmclip&utm_medium=referral [Accessed Friday 16th August, 2024].

The Loss Inside

245 Steve Morse stepping back from the band. Deeppurple.com, https://deeppurple.com/blogs/news/steve-morse-stepping-back-from-the-band [accessed Sunday 18th August 2024].

246 Deep Purple is apolitical, but… The Highway Star, https://www.thehighwaystar.com/news/2022/03/05/deep-purple-is-apolitical-but/ [accessed Saturday 4th February 2023].

247 Ibid.

248 Steve Morse takes hiatus from Deep Purple while his wife battles cancer. Planet Rock, https://hellorayo.co.uk/planet-rock/news/rock-news/steve-morse-deep-purple-hiatus/ [accessed Sunday 18th August 2024].

249 Steve Morse stepping back from the band. Deeppurple.com, https://deeppurple.com/blogs/news/steve-morse-stepping-back-from-the-band [accessed Sunday 18th August 2024].

250 The Steve Morse Band announces first live shows in over a decade. Metal Planet Music, https://metalplanetmusic.com/2023/04/the-steve-morse-band-announces-first-live-shows-in-over-a-decade/ [accessed Monday 19th August 2024].

251 Steve Morse discusses the upcoming Dixie Dregs/Steve Morse Band tour, leaving Deep Purple and more. Sea of Tranquility, https://youtu.be/53PptDgAFuk?si=wGIT2ehucxJjJPTZ

252 Steve Morse Facebook page, 13th September 2023.

253 In Memory of Janine Morse. Steve Morse website, https://stevemorse.com/in-memory-of-janine-morse/ [accessed Tuesday 20th August 2024].

254 Andy West in correspondence with the author.

Epilogue: Better Than Walking Away

255 Stephen Bentley-Klein, interviewed by the author 29th December 2022.

256 Steve Morse On His Departure From Deep Purple: 'They Were Upset For Three To Four Seconds And Then Moved On'. Blabbermouth.net, https://blabbermouth.net/news/steve-morse-on-his-departure-from-deep-purple-they-were-upset-for-three-to-four-seconds-and-then-moved-on [accessed Wednesday 21st August 2024].